As business leaders, we are hyper focused on delivering results. Those KPIs, or metrics, are what propels every organization to constantly push forward and improve. However, those metrics don't magically appear—an environment that fosters that level of growth needs to be implemented and permeate everywhere within the company. This book provides all of the elements for the secret sauce that creates a winning culture, delivers consistent results, and fosters growth. Read the book. Be inspired!

—**JEFFREY HAYZLETT,**
Primetime TV & Podcast Host, Speaker, Author, and Part-Time Cowboy

Leadership is an adventure. Perfect! This is what makes it so exciting! Well done! The book was fantastic! I know I am reading a great leadership book when I find my mind wandering. Not because I am bored, but because I am engaged. I kept finding myself thinking of scenarios, interactions, and ways I could apply what I was reading. Very applicable to leaders at all levels. Great Read!

—**DENNIS RISEMAN,**
Vice President of Sales, PC Connection Business Solutions

Chris Fuller combines information, practical skills, passion and entertaining stories and examples to bring you a book that will make the most seasoned leaders stop and think about leadership. He drills down on the foundational challenges that derail many leaders and empowers the reader with the tools to get intentional in your leadership style. He'll have you flipping from "Thank God it's Friday," to "I can't wait for Monday!"

—**SHEP HYKEN,**
New York Times and Wall Street Journal Best-selling Business Author

In *InSPIRED Leadership*, Chris Fuller has assembled a contemporary tool kit of leadership framework and business maxims that are relevant for every business and team looking to get better results. This book maps out the path to create the systems and culture that will produce Tier 1 actions and results. Invest in your team with this approach and remarkable results will follow!

—MALCOLM O'NEAL,
Vice President of Human Resources, BJ Services

The book is fantastic! Inspired Leadership is an adventure-packed read filled with real-world examples and "Ah-Ha" moments and life-lessons. The book showcases a treasure trove of practical tools for high-performance leaders from someone who really gets it.

—SCOTT DREXLER,
Doctor of Management, Learning Chief-Strategic National Stockpile

Inspired Leadership displays Chris Fuller's influence as a leadership mentor and coach, Chris's real-world business experience and zest for life adventures reveal his passion for excellence in leadership. Whether you are new in your leadership role, a seasoned leader, or a leader struggling under the weight of your responsibility, *this book is for you!* The InSPIRED principles are the key to excellence in leadership and developing strong people leaders. It's what our teams want and need!

—BARRY RUSSELL JR,
Senior Executive, Aviation Industry (36 years)

**YOUR PROVEN PATH
TO REMARKABLE RESULTS**

INSPIRED
LEADERSHIP

Chris Fuller
with Bill Blankschaen

Inspired Leadership: Your Proven Path to Remarkable Results

By Chris Fuller with Bill Blankschaen

Printed in the U.S.A.

© 2020 by Chris Fuller

Published by RightPath Resources

ISBN 978-1-7351259-0-9 (paperback)

Created in collaboration with StoryBuilders (MyStoryBuilders.com)

Cover design by StoryBuilders

To all of the hard working, dedicated leaders who give their very beings to make the world a better place for those around them.

Your modeling of dedication and servant leadership may never be acknowledged by those who reap the benefits, but know it is not lost!

You care more than most, do more than most, and truly make a difference!

You. Inspire. Me.

CONTENTS

CHAPTER 1

YOUR LEADERSHIP ADVENTURE

"Leadership is a privilege to be passionately pursued."

—CHRIS FULLER

Matt found himself mentally drifting, lost in a brain fog on a train to nowhere. He looked out his office window at a nearly empty parking lot and sighed as he glanced at the clock ticking away on the wall—7:30 PM. Another late night at the office. He had promised to be home for dinner tonight. He thought of his wife and three young kids waiting for him—again. By now, they would have given up waiting. If he hurried, maybe he'd make it home in time to tuck the kids into bed and warm up his dinner before knocking out a few more hours of paperwork.

Things didn't use to be this way, he thought. *How did I get so far behind?*

It began with his promotion to management. He had been running nonstop ever since just to feel any hope of survival. And now he had to be back for an early meeting with senior leadership before catching a plane to—where was it again?

What difference does it make, he thought as he headed to the break room and rinsed his coffee cup. *Clearly, I'm not cut out for leadership,* Matt closed the dishwasher door a little too firmly.

When he had first gotten this promotion, he and his wife had been over-the-moon-excited about the opportunity. The extra money meant they could finally get out of their cramped apartment and into a house. They had even hoped to afford private school for the kids. But although they'd bought a house, somehow the money never seemed to stretch to cover school tuition.

In fact, when he did the math, Matt was actually making less per hour than before—but he couldn't exactly ask for his previous job back now, or could he? He had enjoyed that work more. He knew how to do that work. He had the respect of his peers. He could see remarkable results at the end of the day.

Now all he seemed to do was put out endless people and project fires—only to have another blaze up in its place the next day. *Was he even making any difference at all?*

As Matt made his way back toward his office, he passed rows of closed doors and darkened rooms. Sometimes he envied the managers who walked out at five and left yet another hot mess for everyone to deal with the next day. They were content to stagger in and out every day. *They seemed to get away with it,* Matt thought, *so why not try it?* But even as he thought it, Matt knew that just wasn't him. He wanted to do a good job. He wanted to help his people and his company. So why did it have to be so hard?

When he had first been promoted, his boss had told him that although they usually give more in-depth training to new leaders, Matt would need to do on-the-job-training due to budget cuts. At the time, Matt said he understood, but after talking with a few other managers who had been there awhile, Matt realized that tossing new leaders into the deep end was the norm.

Matt shut out any thoughts of tomorrow as he put his laptop into his briefcase and crammed in a stack of folders from his desk and headed out of the office. Jabbing the elevator button for the parking level, he wondered if his time tonight might be better spent browsing LinkedIn for a job he loved that would keep the higher paychecks coming—though he had no idea what that might be. He easily found his car in the nearly empty lot, right next to the big red sign that read, "In Case of Fire, Use Stairs." He smirked as he unlocked the car door and thought, *If only it were that easy to escape this nonstop, always-a-fire-drill way of doing things.* Suddenly, he felt his phone vibrate with a text. He tossed his briefcase into the car and fished out his phone.

It was his boss: "Be ready 2 brief senior team in AM on new strategy we discussed this afternoon. Need to show real data!!" Matt sighed and shook his head before sending a quick "OK." His long night had just gotten longer.

ZOMBIES IN THE WORKPLACE

Unfortunately, if you're a leader in today's business climate, Matt's tale sounds all too familiar. Too many workplaces feel like an episode of *The Walking Dead*—and reruns at that. Zombies, zombies, everywhere, and the hits keep coming. Matt dealt with it by putting in twice as much time, believing hard work and long hours are the answer. Other managers left at closing time, no matter what messes they had created or avoided during the day. Neither approach helps solve the problem.

But is there any hope? Even when struggling to lead well, organizational momentum works against leaders to produce the same outcomes: less engagement and lower productivity. Leaders and their teams stumble into work on Monday with one eye on the clock and the other on Friday. And the sad truth is that both the workplace zombies and their families feel the effect.

These zombified workplaces know few walls or borders. According to the 2017 Gallup *State of the Global Workplace* study, global productivity is in decline. This extensive annual study covering three years and drawing data from 195 countries around the world serves as the benchmark for measuring business success and productivity around the world. It tells a rather bleak story. Global worldwide employee engagement is at *only 15%*. That means a shocking 85% of employees are NOT engaged at work! That's a lot of zombies.

A whopping 67% of employees are indifferent at best, just punching the clock for a paycheck, while another 18% are actively disengaged. In the US and Canada, engagement rises to 31%, but that still leaves almost 70% of the workforce NOT engaged on a daily basis—or worse, actively undermining the company where they work.

This disengagement costs organizations a lot in revenue and productivity. Companies who measured in the highest quartile of employee engagement—as compared to the bottom quartile—saw significant real-world improvements in customer metrics, sales, profitability, and productivity, while drastically reducing absenteeism, turnover, shrinkage, and even employee safety incidents. It turns out that when people are engaged at work, they do more, complain less, and make a healthier contribution to the bottom line.

But what about those who are not actively engaged? As the largest group, they're also the ones most directly affecting results. Unlike toxic employees, who can be easy to spot, disengaged people often hide in plain sight. As the Gallup study notes, "These workers are not hostile or disruptive. They do not hate their job or set out to wreak havoc. They are indifferent and will put the time—but not the energy or passion—into their role." These camouflaged zombies make it difficult to get anything done. Innovation, creativity, productivity—basically everything needed to improve organizational performance—slows to a blind stagger. In short, disengaged workers cause massive losses in productivity—between $450 and $500 billion a year.[1]

So if engaged employees result in more of everything organizations want and less of what they dread, what is the key factor that determines an employee's level of engagement? *Leadership*—and the culture it creates.

Engagement is ultimately a leadership problem. When it comes to job satisfaction, most employees cite factors the leader or organization can control but chooses to ignore. Indirectly, or directly, it comes back to leaders who fail to lead people to a better, more inspired performance. People won't give their discretionary effort to leaders they don't like or respect.

Leaders bear responsibility for the disengagement crisis. Leadership is both the cause and the solution. To improve underperforming team members and retain top performers, leaders must improve how they engage and equip people. They must behave in ways that earn respect and make them worth following. What they do shapes the culture of an organization. It's not that most leaders don't care, they just don't know how to lead. They've never been properly equipped and empowered. Most leaders get promoted because they achieved results in one setting and were rewarded with a position of leadership without being handed a leadership manual.

They get tossed into the deep end of a position that requires a totally new skill set. They start doing what got them there—only to discover that the new level requires a different recipe for success—and no one has told them the secret ingredients. Frustration, burnout, turnover, and poor performance soon follow. Technical skill sets and IQ, as important as they may be, don't automatically translate into better leadership. In fact, some of the worst leaders can be the smartest people in the room.

Maybe it's time we started thinking differently about preparing leaders to lead? What if instead of accepting the high costs of disengagement or blaming it on the employees, we equipped leaders fully so they could embrace leadership as an adventure? What if we taught them how to create an InSPIRED culture that produces truly remarkable results, the kind of bottom-line, real-world success that gets talked about for years to come? How might that kind of high-performance culture impact the underlying success factors that lead to a decisive competitive advantage: employee retention, leadership vitality, and customer service?

If culture eats strategy for breakfast, then getting the day-to-day culture right will pay massive dividends for leaders and the companies they serve. InSPIRED leadership transforms zombies into raving fans of you and your brand, engaged employees who eagerly anticipate Monday *and* enjoy the weekend to the fullest.

HOW ZOMBIFIED ARE YOU?

The truth is that no one sets out to create a zombified workplace culture. No one searches for a job where they can be disengaged. Yet here we are. The numbers don't lie. Most people are not only uninspired by the workplace experience, they're barely surviving. It feels as if no one understands or cares about the pain. They get no understanding from the boss, who's just trying to keep his or her own head above water. They get no understanding from direct reports who are resigned to going through the motions to get a paycheck. And to top it all off, their peers are working their own agendas to fight for the headcount they need to survive.

On the home front, kids' soccer games, dinner with a significant other, or just some down time to relax and recharge, all get cut for the endless fire drills at work. Bottom line: people feel judged at home for working too much, judged at work for not working fast enough, and judged by their direct reports for running a sweatshop—all while their peers elbow them on the way up the corporate ladder.

Diet and exercise get sacrificed. The brain becomes locked in hyperresponsive alert mode, killing creativity and focus. Sleep vanishes. Relationships shrivel and die. But the boss just keeps asking for more. So people find a way to cope—food addictions, alcohol, drugs of all sorts, marital affairs, becoming a zombie to protect oneself—the list can be pretty long. Then at some point, the switch gets tripped and life implodes.

I get it. Maybe you do, too. I've been there, done that—and got the tattoo. When I was a younger leader and father of two young children, I poured myself into building a construction company. And when I say *poured*, I mean I was a human *doing*, not a human *being*. The guy whose company I was helping to build was a demanding leader who used negative motivation to manipulate people. After I would kill myself to achieve the impossible, he would say things like, "I was hoping for more. Maybe you're not as good as I thought you were. Let me know if you want out. I have guys who will take your place tomorrow."

So I'd double down and do more. He would even pit one of us against the other. It was a workplace mess, but one that may sound all too familiar to you.

Over the course of several years, I helped him grow that company from $600,000 to $21 million with annual revenue streaming in from seven different offices. Unfortunately, I wasn't wise in how I set up the deal I had with him. After years of living the zombie life, I got only a fraction of the multiple six-figures I had been promised with an invitation to "sue me" for the rest of it.

And the results I did achieve for him came at a high price. I was running all the time, always on, and traveling nonstop. I packed on the pounds, settling for the easy option of burgers and fries, too exhausted to think of eating better or exercising. Because I'd been taking grief all day at work, when I got home I created spousal disconnect and fights about, well, everything—and nothing—all at the same time.

Even when I was technically home, I'm ashamed to say that I wasn't truly present. When I walked in the front door, the kids would run to me, wanting to play—but I would strike the Heisman pose, stiff-arming them so I could squeeze in one more phone call while juggling my laptop loaded with precious spreadsheets. I shudder to think of all the times they ate without me, then went to bed while I kept working long into the night. I pretty much defined "uninspired" for far too long in my career.

But life has a way of helping us see things clearly eventually. The only question is: What price will we pay for that clarity?

Fast forward many years and numerous leadership and life lessons to July 4, 2009. Out of nowhere, my son Josh's military base in Afghanistan got hit by a Taliban attack. As the base started getting shelled, one of Josh's friends, Army PFC Aaron E. Fairbairn, took a direct hit. PFC Justin Casillas rushed to save him, carrying him toward the medic tent—when they both took a second direct hit. Both men, my sons' buddies, died instantly. Then a truck loaded with explosives drove full speed toward the main gate.

Already under mortar attack, Josh's military unit knew they had to stop the approaching 5,000-kilogram truck bomb from completing its deadly mission. My son ran to the tower where his team of brave soldiers focused everything on stopping that driver. The radio operator called for Blackhawk helicopter support knowing this was likely their last stand.

The truck made it through the first checkpoint, but Josh's unit shot the driver before the truck got through the second and final gate. Even so, the truck still exploded. The Taliban had installed a remote detonator on the truck activated with a "dead man's switch." At the time of the blast, Josh was partially shielded by the tower, or he too would have died instantly. As it was, he was blown backward and suffered a severe concussion after being knocked unconscious.

Within a couple of years, his brother would face similarly deadly scenarios in the Helmand province. Had either son not come home, I don't know how badly I would have beaten myself up over not being present for them when I had the chance. But I know the price I paid for living an uninspired life wasn't anywhere close to worth it.

How many boys and girls go without moms and dads because marriages end due to workplace stress or a parent stays late at work? How many kids seek affirmation elsewhere through substance abuse, sex, or relationships that lead them astray, when all they really want are parents who choose to be fully present in their lives? How much human carnage ensues because parents come home stressed out from work and fuss at the kids instead of investing the time to nurture them? How many kids ask Siri or Google for life knowledge, rather than seeking it in the critical parental context?

Why such horrors? Where does life disengagement begin? It starts when we refuse the invitation to lead others in an inspired way. It worsens when we come to believe we must hold onto a job at all cost. Ultimately, if we don't architect an inspired plan for ourselves and the people we lead, we contribute to and create real tragedy.

THE CALL TO ADVENTURE

The way I see it, life is an adventure to be lived, not a crisis to be survived. Leadership is a privilege to be passionately pursued. I've experienced leadership at every level imaginable, from being a first-time leader thrust unprepared into a position to working in the trenches alongside C-Suite leaders at Fortune 500 companies who feel overwhelmed—but think they can't afford to let anyone know.

When I started working in sales at an electronics store at the age of eighteen, I got noticed after I blew by everyone else. Consequently, the management there did what gets done to most people who produce: they assumed I could lead and promoted me into sales management. They seemed to think that if I was good at sales, imagine what I could do when I cloned five other people to sell just like I did!

I eagerly threw myself into my new leadership position—and face-planted in the first week. I planned an awesome first meeting, but not one of my former peers even showed up. Right then, I knew I had a lot to learn about leadership. I was ill-equipped to take responsibility, and that lack of training set me up for failure.

I committed to a leadership growth journey and started consuming books on leadership. I got my accounting degree and became Director of Information Systems for an aircraft fastener company. Then the guy I mentioned earlier approached me about helping him grow the construction company. In spite of many missteps in that experience, I learned about growing people in the sales process, logistics, distribution, and project management.

My passion for helping people learn and grow led to my partnering with my brother to invest in an instructional design business. Our first major client was The John Maxwell Company. I helped John develop and deploy relevant resources for corporate leadership training. Over the past fifteen years, as the business scaled and morphed into more leadership consulting than instructional design, I've had the privilege of working with numerous organizations, from start-ups to Fortune 500 companies and many brands that are household names.

> Leadership is a privilege to be passionately pursued.

All the while, I was building my own intellectual property that reflected my unique vision for leadership as an adventure to be embraced. I've always been intentional about building adventure into my life. Rock climbing, dirt bikes, supersport motorcycles, skydiving, scuba diving, deep-sea fishing—you name it, I've done it.

Adventure inspires me. It lights me up and helps me fully engage life. As a result, I've experienced a few adventures most people would never attempt. I've traveled to Nome, Alaska to mush an Iditarod dogsled team. I've choppered into base camp at Mount Everest to be as near as possible to the top of the world. I attended the America's Cup sailing competition to watch those engineering marvels fly over the water. I went out in a retired *Stars and Stripes* boat to try my own hand as part of the crew of an America's Cup boat.

Every time I engaged one of these experiences, I learn more about leadership. I returned inspired, ready to tackle the next great leadership adventure. I'll share some of those stories in the pages that follow, but it's important for you to know that you don't have to jump out of planes or fly to the highest summits to live and lead in an inspired fashion. Your people just need you to show them the InSPIRED pathway.

THE INSPIRED LEADERSHIP PATHWAY

According to Gallup, employees "are now driven more than ever by mission and purpose and require a workplace culture that delivers it." People want to know their work has a deeper purpose they can tap into every day. This purpose makes them want to get out of bed and go to work. I think of it as an Ethos of Impact—people want to be inspired by the work *and you.*

But how? The tyranny of the urgent, the muscle memory of the organization, and the status quo can make change extremely difficult. In mature organizations, bureaucracy and silos can create distance and encourage indifference. Meanwhile, companies that have grown quickly also face challenges to creating inspired culture—*scale* and *speed.*

It starts by imagining a workplace where people are not zombies but fully-engaged, energized, and passionate people. As they leave your company for the day, they head home to their families and significant others better people than when they arrived that morning. That's what an InSPIRED culture does. And those people who go home full of life each day can't wait to return on Monday to fully engage in *your* InSPIRED mission. It's not fantasy. It *can* be reality for your workplace.

> People want to be inspired by you.

So how do you get there? Engage the leadership adventure using The InSPIRED Leadership Pathway. I developed this proven pathway over many years of working in the trenches alongside leaders of all backgrounds in a wide variety of organizations.

The letters of the word *inspired* form an acrostic of the seven areas leaders and organizations must address to achieve remarkable results:

INtentional. An InSPIRED culture begins to form when you get intentional. Some companies and leaders succeed without ever understanding why. But how can you replicate what you don't understand? Excellence is never an accident.

Service. More than ever, service matters. An InSPIRED culture serves both external and internal customers. How people experience your team or organization over time becomes their expectation. Their expectation of you becomes your brand. Is your brand one that serves others well, or is it a self-serving brand? Do you even know?

Passion. What fires you up? What passions fuel your best performance? Inspiration may influence you, but passion moves you and motivates the people you lead. At the end of the day, it doesn't matter what your product or service is—if you're in leadership, you're in the people business. And people run on passion.

Integration. Everything is connected in your organization. But how well do all the parts and pieces work together? The gears and sprockets that make up the inner workings will determine whether you produce inspired results or the clock expires on your results. If you've ever found yourself thinking, "It really shouldn't be this hard," then you know the pain of disintegration.

Real. As much as business leaders focus on hard data like production numbers and the bottom line, real people touch everything and determine long-term success. Everyone is wired for greatness, but not everyone is wired for greatness in the same areas. Consequently, the best leaders develop a team of people who lead where they're strong and team where they're weak. To do that, you must first get to know the people you lead in a real way.

Execution. Why do you need to inspire? To get results. And to get results, your team has to execute. If you don't actually get things done with an accountability cadence, all your work becomes merely a relational exercise. The reason you need to be intentional, service-focused, passionate, integrated, and real is so you can execute with excellence to achieve optimal results.

Develop. Once you achieve excellence, the question becomes: can you sustain it tomorrow, next week, and next year? The best leaders know they can't stand still—they must continue to develop. So how do you and your team do that? By choosing to get better every day. Leaders must choose to develop continually.

In the pages to follow, we'll unpack and apply each of these components to help you embrace your own leadership adventure—from wherever you are to wherever you need to go.

LEAVING THE ZOMBIES BEHIND

The InSPIRED Leadership Pathway isn't a fire-and-forget action. It's a process. Becoming an InSPIRED leader and organization won't happen tomorrow, but it can happen if you choose to start changing today. The first thing you may have to change is your beliefs, because beliefs drive behavior:

- Do you believe you *can* impact the workforce culture?

- Do you believe you *can* create an InSPIRED microculture within the existing culture?

- Do you believe you *can* lead your team and organization to produce extraordinary results consistently?

- Do you believe people *can* break out of the zombified stupor and truly enjoy coming to work on Monday?

- Do you believe you *can* experience a workplace culture that sends people home at the end of the day energized and ready to engage a full life with family and friends?

You may be thinking, *Chris, can we really just wave a magic wand and suddenly enjoy an inspired workplace?* Of course not. You must lead well. I want to help you lead your team, and perhaps your entire company culture, to a place where you and everyone else enjoys a fulfilling life, both at and outside of work. The InSPIRED leadership adventure is all about pursuing the opportunity to do meaningful work with great people who work an inspired process.

> The InSPIRED leadership adventure is all about pursuing the opportunity to do meaningful work with great people who work an inspired process.

Now, if you're ready to stop following the zombies and become an InSPIRED leader, no matter what your current position or title, keep reading. Because the InSPIRED adventure begins, right now.

TOOL KIT

Summary

- Unlike toxic employees, who can be easy to spot, disengaged people often hide in plain sight.

- When it comes to job satisfaction, most employees cite factors the leader or organization can control but chooses to ignore.

- If culture eats strategy for breakfast, then getting the day-to-day culture right will pay massive dividends for leaders and the companies they serve.

- InSPIRED leadership transforms zombies into raving fans of you and your brand, engaged, customer-centric employees who eagerly anticipate Monday and enjoy the weekend to the fullest.

- The numbers don't lie. Most people are not only uninspired by the workplace experience, they're barely surviving.

- Life is an adventure to be lived, not a crisis to be survived. Leadership is a privilege to be passionately pursued.

Startling Statistics

- Global worldwide employee engagement is only 15%. That means a shocking 85% of employees are NOT engaged at work!

- A whopping 67% of employees are indifferent at best, just punching the clock for a paycheck, while another 18% are actively disengaged.

- In the US and Canada, almost 70% of the people in the workplace are NOT engaged on a daily basis—or worse, actively undermining the company where they work.

- Disengaged workers cause massive losses in productivity—between $450 and $500 billion a year.

Action Steps

- **Evaluate your zombie level.** If you're struggling to keep your head above water—or burying your head in the sand, you may not realize how zombified you are. Take an honest look at where you are in your leadership journey. Are you faking it, but not making it? Are you struggling to get by?

- **Embrace the adventure.** Think about why you wanted to be a leader in the first place. It probably wasn't just to make money; it's usually about impact. It's time to reconnect with what you loved about leadership. Write down all the benefits that come from being a good leader—for you, your team, and your company. Then display that list prominently where you'll see it and be motivated every day.

- **Get intentional about your leadership.** Leadership may mean saying no to some things so you can say yes to the best. It's time to put mediocre behind you and strive for the excellence only you can deliver. Make a commitment to yourself to work through The InSPIRED Leadership Pathway and intentionally apply the lessons to reclaim your leadership adventure.

CHAPTER 2

WHEN THE DREAM BECOMES A NIGHTMARE

"One way to get the most out of life is to look upon it as an adventure."

—WILLIAM FEATHER

We are all wired for adventure. You may be more or less risk averse than others, but we all want to experience the highest summits—whatever those summits may look like for you. It's when those summits call to you that you discover what you're really made of.

Real-life adventure inspires me personally. It makes me feel alive. And when it comes to settings for adventure, one setting stands high above the rest—Mount Everest. At 29,035 feet above sea level, Everest is quite literally the tallest summit on earth, the ultimate pinnacle of the mountain-climbing world.

Everest resisted all attempts to summit until Sir Edmund Hillary and Sherpa Tenzing Norgay did it in 1953. It's not a feat for the faint of heart. As veteran Everest climber Ed Viesturs describes the experience, "You don't assault Everest. You sneak up on it, and then get the hell outta there."[2] In spite of, or perhaps because of, the danger, the summit beckons to bold adventurers. George Mallory, a British mountaineer who participated in the first three British climbing expeditions in the early 1920s was once famously asked, "Why do you want to climb Mount Everest?" His classic response, "Because it's there."

But having the desire to tackle a mountain that has claimed nearly 300 lives isn't enough. For one thing, the average expedition costs around $65,000. It takes nearly two and a half months to get there, become acclimated to the higher altitude, and make the ascent. And it all has to happen during a tight window each year in late April and early May. Before April, the bitter cold makes climbing nearly impossible. After June, the monsoon season begins.

Climbers usually begin their trek by flying to Kathmandu, the capital city of Nepal. From there, adventurers take a short flight to Lukla—with an elevation of nearly 9,000 feet. With a short runway of only 1,729 feet, it's labeled the world's most dangerous airport. Most climbers spend the next two weeks trekking about thirty-eight miles up to Base Camp at 17,600 feet, more than three miles above sea level. The thin air at that altitude demands that everyone take the time to acclimate if they want to stay. But the summit of Everest is still two miles higher.

During the spring climbing window, Everest Base Camp typically houses around 300 people, including climbers, sherpas, cook staff, doctors, scientists and expedition leaders. The climbers spend weeks there, taking day hikes into the higher elevations to transport supplies and become familiar with the treacherous landscape, blistering winds, icy crevasses, and decreased oxygen levels. The time invested waiting for the ideal climbing window isn't wasted; it's critical to achieve the desired result—summit the world's highest mountain, the most inhospitable place on earth and live to tell the story.

From Everest Base Camp, the next steps on the most popular Southeast Ridge or South Col Route are a series of designed stages which bring climbers closer to the peak while getting their bodies ready for the grueling challenge. The very first challenging stage is crossing the Khumbu Icefall, a jumbled mass of ice that can only be crossed with the aid of jerry-rigged ropes and ladders. This shifting landscape must often be crossed several times by climbers moving supplies using duct-taped ladders to transverse crevasses that seemingly have no bottom. Ropes and ladders must be checked daily as the ice constantly shifts, sometimes as much as three feet each day.

Once across the icefall, climbers reach Camp I, elevation 19,900 feet. The next stage runs through a glacial valley known as Western Cwm and ends at Camp II, elevation 21,300 feet.

The fourth stage requires climbers to tackle the imposing Lhotse Face, a sheer wall of ice that can only be climbed using fixed ropes. If they make it past that challenge, they arrive at Camp III, elevation 24,500 feet. From there, climbers trek through the Geneva Spur to reach Camp IV or South Col.

At 26,000 feet above sea level, it's the last camp for climbers before they begin the final push to the summit of Mount Everest. Conditions at this camp are brutal. It's known as the Death Zone because of the frigid temps, high winds, and lack of oxygen.

Most climbers waken early for the final push to the summit, often setting out hours before daylight. They must summit by 2 PM or face the deadly prospect of attempting to climb back down in the dark—a feat few have attempted and even fewer survived. On the way up, usually with the aid of oxygen tanks to keep their brain functioning clearly, climbers travel to The Balcony, a platform at 27,700 feet where they can rest briefly before moving on to The Cornice Traverse, a horizontal face of rock and snow. Then they must ascend The Hillary Step by way of fixed ropes one person at a time.

As hard as it may be to believe, traffic jams on good climbing days can doom an expedition without coordination between teams. However, if a climber can navigate all of those challenges, he or she can stand on the very top of the world. Yet for all the time, money, energy, and effort, most climbers can only spend less than an hour there before beginning the descent, which is every bit as harrowing and hazardous as the ascent.

Needless to say, no one ever arrives at the highest summit by accident. It requires intentional planning and action.

SHORTCUT TO THE TOP

On April 8, 2015, I had my own opportunity to experience Everest. I had been in India meeting with a client and realized I was probably as close to the world's greatest adventure as I was ever going to get. I had my destination in mind but needed a plan to get there. So, I booked a flight to Kathmandu with the goal of at least getting to Everest Base Camp.

I learned that the hike from Lukla to Base Camp takes around two weeks. I had three days—and the wrong boots. So I chose to take a shortcut. I convinced a pilot to chopper me all the way up through the Himalayas to Everest Base Camp. Even with a stop at the world's deadliest airport in Lukla to refuel, it seemed like a good plan. In a period of about 6 hours, I traveled from Noida, India (elevation 656 feet) to Kathmandu, Nepal (4,593 feet) to Lukla Airport (9,000 feet). After stopping to refuel there, I excitedly jumped back on board to head to Everest Base Camp (17,500 feet). I was on an incredible adventure!

I was a prime example of knowing just enough to be dangerous.

As we crested the majestic peaks, I saw the small city of tents that make up Base Camp. As I saw the flags whipping in the breeze, my excitement mounted. In a few moments, I'd stand at Base Camp, look across the Khumbu Icefall, and stare up at the top of the world. When my feet touched the ground, it was everything I had hoped for—amazing and exhilarating.

Then the sinus pressure kicked in. It didn't take long for a splitting headache to follow. I had given myself hours to the acclimate to the thin air. Without preparation, my body could only take so much. My trip to what was almost the top of the world lasted less than an hour.

Although my brief journey was an adventure of sorts, it was nothing like the adventure Sir Edmund Hillary had scaling Everest. It couldn't be, because I had been dropped in, unprepared for the experience. I had no chance of summiting Everest or even staying long enough to watch the sun go down. It was fun while it lasted, don't get me wrong, but I was in over my head without proper training, equipment, and an intentional plan.

WHEN THE DREAM BECOMES A NIGHTMARE

My brief Everest experience mirrors the leadership journey of many well-intentioned leaders who get promoted without adequate training and preparation. They get dropped into Base Camp after a quick helicopter ride. They're pumped to get climbing. They're amazed and exhilarated, but quickly realize they're having trouble breathing the rarified air. All the excitement in the world won't help.

But unlike my experience, no one really gets the option of heading back down to a comfortable place once they've been promoted, do they? So they rapidly feel stuck, dazed, and frustrated and the leadership dream becomes a nightmare.

If your leadership dream has become a nightmare, let me give you some good news: *it's not your fault.* I coach and counsel leaders all the time who are exactly where you are right now. Just like when I was promoted into sales management without training, you may have been promoted to a position without being prepared. On one hand, you can't blame the leaders above you who saw your potential and wanted you to lead. And you probably can lead well—with the right preparation. The fact that you're reading this book, after all, proves you have an interest in acclimating for the climb.

Even so, it can be incredibly frustrating to feel like you're out of oxygen but are afraid someone will find out. Organizations the world over are filled with frustrated, overwhelmed leaders who are doing their best but not achieving success.

As I lead corporate training sessions, I often encounter glazed looks from people who have become numb to the day-to-day pressures instead of leading the drive to relieve those pressures. It's as if they never acclimated to the leadership altitude and are simply trying to survive on a fraction of the oxygen they really need to thrive. It's not uncommon for me to find cautious, skeptical, even sarcastic "that'll-be-the-day" reactions to the thought of an inspired workplace culture. Sure, people want it—and they'd even be willing to step up and help get it done—but experience has taught

> If your leadership dream has become a nightmare, let me give you some good news: it's not your fault.

them to keep their heads down, their mouths shut, and just grind out the work.

For new leaders, this jaded thinking from grizzled veterans can be hard to understand. *Shiny ideals are great, but when the rubber meets the road, you'll see how it really is around here.* And so the zombification of the workforce continues. Ultimately, the culture fills with burned out, used up, and exhausted people—perhaps people like you—who really want to perform at a higher level, but have become frustrated and disengaged. They don't know how to be a catalyst for positive change.

If you're like me, however, you refuse to accept that bleak status quo. If, in spite of your frustration, you think, *There's got to be a better way,* I have good news for you! InSPIRED Leadership can create an inspired culture that encourages inspired employees and makes an inspired difference in the world. That sort of inspired adventure isn't a dream. It can become a reality for you, your team, or your organization.

4 INSPIRED QUESTIONS

Whether you are just starting your leadership journey or have been in leadership most of your career, one thing is always true: the leadership adventure can overwhelm. Like quarterbacks in football, leaders get more than their share of both credit and blame. It can be easy to feel you're giving a Herculean effort but still feel under-resourced and victimized.

But what are you going to do—quit? Maybe you've got a mortgage, a spouse, kids, and a whole list of other reasons you need the paycheck. When you accepted the promotion, you likely elevated your lifestyle to match your new income. And, if you're honest, there's likely some ego involved. After all, none of us like to fail or admit we don't know what we're doing.

On top of all of that, American corporate culture tends to value action, not planning or (gasp!) pre-planning. We prefer to make our mistakes in real-time, rather than wait for a prototype. The consequences of action without intentional forethought can be devastating. We think we boarded the scenic Orient Express to the leadership summit, but instead, we're on a bullet train headed for an abyss.

It's very likely you have unrealistic requirements, fuzzy expectations, and impossible deadlines—and no one prepared you to handle any of them. Oh, and if you were recently promoted from within, you're probably one of the top performers on the team, and now your spot is vacant, and you may feel the expectation to continue to be the top individual contributor even as you try to fulfill your new role as a leader. Unfortunately, that math doesn't work. It won't be long before you run out of gas. You're on the trail to being a zombie.

Fortunately, if your dream *has* become a nightmare, there is a way to reconnect to your inspiration, fuel your growth, and start working a more effective process. But before we work on your inspired process, I suggest you start with you—the inspired person. The best way I have found to do this is by considering four InSPIRED questions.

1. WHAT INSPIRES YOU?

I understand what it feels like to feel unappreciated at your job, to lose sight of what inspires you and go through the motions. I know what it can feel like when you're carrying the weight of the world on your shoulders and falling short as a leader for your team. But I've also learned to tap into inspiration.

When you hear about my Everest story or that I've mushed with dogs in Alaska, you might think I just like to go to cold places. The truth is I've learned to seek out adventure no matter where I am. I find adventures to be inspiring, but they may just sound crazy to you. That's ok. It doesn't matter what I find inspirational, but what inspires you?

> Reengage the leadership adventure by reconnecting with what inspires you.

What lights you up? Your inspiration is as unique as you are. Is it music? Is it art? Is it architecture? When you go to a theater for a performance, are you just as inspired by the architecture and the design of the stage as you are by the power of music, drama, or spoken word? Or do you find your inspiration in nature or simply getting out in the fresh air? Maybe it's strolling through national forests or kayaking down the Colorado River.

Do patriotism and a passion for country stir you? Do you stand a little taller as the flag goes by, or are you moved by great stories of selfless sacrifice? What about the story of some guys from Dallas who headed to Houston with their boats to help after Hurricane Harvey struck in 2017? Does selfless sacrifice inspire you?

Or are you inspired by the human condition? What about the amputee boy who can now walk, and even run, because somebody designed running blades? When you look at his beaming face, are you inspired to want to become the engineer who creates more products that unleash the human potential?

Are you moved by committed educators or medical caregivers, doctors, nurses, and healers who invest years of their lives to make a difference in others' lives? What about the story of Sara Tucholsky tearing her ACL while running the bases on her only college home run? Opposing team members Mallory Holtman and Liz Wallace made sure she made it around the bases, touching every base.[3]

What about strapping an airplane engine to a Formula 1 car and the engineering required to fly at 300-plus miles an hour while navigating tricky S-curves? Do you admire the power and beauty of such a machine?

Are you inspired by story? Do grand tales move you to learn and grow so you can live a story worthy of being told someday? If so, what kind of stories move you?

All of these can be inspiring in their own way, but here's the most important question: *What fuels your life?*

Maybe a better question would be this: *what fire inside have you allowed to fade?* We all get busy. Life happens. I get it. But life is too short to let those passions die. Uninspired leaders produce uninspired leadership. It's time to reignite those flames and release that inspirational energy.

I invite you to reengage the leadership adventure by reconnecting with what inspires you. Tap into what lifts your spirits and moves you to think bigger, bolder, and more beautiful ideas.

Inspiration is all about being stimulated to do or feel something deeper. The reason organizations are filled with walking zombies is because those zombies have lost the ability to feel much of anything at all. The more we stay on that treadmill of organizational muscle memory—doing what we've always done but expecting different results—the less inspired any of us act.

It may be that you are so far removed from an inspired place right now that you've forgotten what it feels like to be inspired. If that's the case, I encourage you to pause and think about what inspires you.

Inspiration is electric. It can stimulate you to become a better person and a better leader. It prompts creativity that enables you to see problems differently and solve them in intuitive ways. When people are inspired, time moves quickly. They stay focused, get in the groove, and enjoy work because it's no longer drudgery, but elevated and important.

You may have to go back to your childhood and think about things you used to love. Children don't think about whether or not someone else is watching; they just do things that make them happy. They play in the mud. They take a bite out of the middle of their sandwich and smear peanut butter and jelly on their cheeks. They dance and laugh and wiggle with internal joy. When you were a kid, what did you love to do? Was it sports, music, art, imagination? How long has it been since you've used those inspiration muscles?

> How long has it been since you've used those inspiration muscles?

Growing up in Texas, I spent most summers outdoors. I would head out in the morning with friends to ride bikes or explore. Many times I didn't return until the sun went down. We found undeveloped fields that became our canvas for imagination. We baited string rods to catch crawdads in the nearby creeks. We intentionally sought out each new day's adventure!

Tapping into what inspires you is the first step to becoming an InSPIRED leader. So if it's been a while since you've connected with what inspires you, now's your chance to remember what it is—*and why.*

2. WHO INSPIRES YOU?

Inspiration is contagious. Inspirational people have a way of affecting our souls and changing our thinking. We all model our lives after somebody. As kids, we model what we see in our parents and older siblings. Our word choices, actions, attitudes, and way of viewing the world all are shaped by what we see modeled for us. As adults, we encounter more and different viewpoints, we get to choose new patterns to imitate and replicate.

There is no one right way to achieve success in life. Mohammed Ali rose to athletic greatness and inspired millions. Oprah Winfrey started out as a small-town newsperson and became a media mogul. Mother Teresa served the poor in the worst conditions. Gandhi, Steve Jobs, Malala from Pakistan, Nelson Mandela, Martin Luther King, Jr., Albert Einstein—the list goes on. Each of these people had drastically different personalities, values, and vision, yet they all inspired millions.

> Inspiration is contagious.

One of the first people to inspire me and speak deeply into my life was a guy named Jim. He put a John Maxwell book in one hand and Stephen Covey's *The Seven Habits of Highly Effective People* in the other and began to teach me about leadership. As one of my first mentors, he told me he believed in me and saw amazing talent in me. It changed me and made me want to elevate my game.

So who inspires you? You may have never given it much thought. I encourage you to pause and consider it now. Who are your heroes? What leaders inspire you? Great leaders have a way of bringing out the best in people. They encourage, uplift, and inspire. As you think about leaders who've inspired you, ask what it is about them that speaks to you on a deep level. What is it about them that energizes you and makes you want to make them proud?

> Imitation isn't just the sincerest form of flattery, it's also the quickest way to get remarkable results.

When you know who inspires you, you can identify the individual components that make them who they are and find things to replicate in your own life and leadership. Everyone's life can be a lesson if you understand how to let it teach you. Imitation isn't just the sincerest form of flattery, it's also the quickest way to get remarkable results.

Why reinvent the wheel when so much of what you need to live an inspired life has already been modeled for you? Find awesome and copy it.

You don't have to know someone personally to gain wisdom from them. You can engage some of the best mentors in the pages of books or via an online course or video. Use it all. Read voraciously, take notes, and apply what you learn to your own life to equip you for your own leadership journey.

3. CAN BRANDS BE INSPIRATIONAL?

What about brands? Can they be inspirational? What is the brand you serve? Think for a moment before you answer. You may sell one thing but deliver another. When Steve Jobs introduced the iPod, he sold a metal box with a microprocessor, small screen, and a clickable wheel. But what did he deliver? A thousand songs in your pocket. That small piece of hardware changed the way people consumed music. It might be retro cool now to buy albums on vinyl or even cassette, but a thousand songs in your pocket was transformational in 2001, helping pave the way for the iPhone and establish Apple as a global monolith.

Brands clearly have an identity, much like a person, but do they always inspire? As a leader in an organization, you are a torchbearer for your brand. The things you say and do reflect on the brand. The NFL for years has talked about the shield when referring to their logo. They have high standards for what they want their brand to be. That's why players get fined for wearing the wrong cleats or something that doesn't match the uniform. It's seen as disrespectful to the shield. The NFL has a brand code that it expects its players to live up to and abide by. Unfortunately, however, many fans feel the NFL has been inspiring in the wrong direction lately. Right or wrong, the League has paid a price for that perception.

Some brands, like Apple, become status symbols. Others like Tom's Shoes and Patagonia become outlets for causes the owners and employees can support. Now more than ever, brands have a say in how they are perceived in the marketplace. Dove, a Unilever Skincare brand, launched a campaign several years ago called "Real Beauty." You may remember the ads. It began when they "put six women in their underwear on a billboard in Times Square and challenged conventional norms of beauty imagery." These women weren't famous supermodels with recognizable faces. They were women of all shapes, sizes, and skin tones and showed that Dove products were for everyone. It was a risky proposition that could have backfired, but according to Rob Candelino, Vice President of Brand Building for Unilever Skincare, the campaign transformed the company's image. Candelino said that the billboard "was so groundbreaking and profoundly *inspiring* to women" that they were flooded with positive feedback.[4]

Think about the following brands: Zappos, Starbucks, Target, Salvation Army, Red Cross, Tesla, Google, Disney, Chick-fil-A, Walmart, Home Depot, and Amazon. Do they evoke a positive or negative reaction in you? Would you want to work with these brands? Why? Why not? What have these brands done that sticks in your mind and causes a reaction? What cultures do you think these brands have inside the company's walls? Some are listed among the top places to work. Others are frequently defending their culture and treatment of employees. Are their employees happy, highly regarded, frustrated, exhausted?

Now consider this: just as you have a reaction to these brands, your customers and the marketplace have a reaction to *your* organization's brand. Your company brand is and will be known for something. It may be the lowest cost, the highest quality, reliability, luxury, economy, sportiness, value, or humor. The list of possibilities is nearly endless. How your company is perceived by your customers and stakeholders who view you from the outside is shaped by the way you build your culture on the inside. An InSPIRED culture intentionally built by InSPIRED leaders produces an InSPIRED brand.

Whether you lead an organization of millions, a division of thousands, or a team of a few, your leadership can inspire—or exasperate—the brand you lead. Yes, that's right. Even a small team has a brand identity. You can decide to be an inspirational leader or an exasperating leader who shapes that brand in either direction.

If you choose to do nothing about your leadership style, you'll naturally become exasperating to those you lead. No one wants to follow someone who simply goes through the motions. What do you want your brand to be? What type of leader will you need to become to create a team that embodies that brand?

4. IS YOUR PERSONAL LEADERSHIP BRAND INSPIRATIONAL?

Everyone knows what it's like to work under bad leadership. It frays our nerves, frustrates our efforts, and leads to burnout. Yet most leaders think they're doing a good job of leading. The zombification of employees and extraordinarily high levels of disengagement in the workforce today (almost 70% in the US and Canada!) tell a different story. People won't give maximum effort to a leader they don't like or respect.

So how inspirational are you? Do you know you have a brand of your own? You are known by what you do—good, bad, or ugly. Does your personal brand inspire or exasperate? One of the biggest issues I see with sincere leaders is a lack of self-awareness. They've either never taken the time to learn about themselves, or they're just paddling as fast as possible to keep the ship moving forward.

InSPIRED leaders, on the other hand, are extremely self-aware. They know themselves inside and out, or at least have a plan for self-discovery. They know their personalities and their strengths. They have a plan to use both to motivate and empower others. They also understand their weaknesses and have a plan to shore them up. Plus, they know where they want to go, seldom becoming stagnant. They create opportunity and train others to become inspiring leaders.

This book will be most beneficial to you if you are willing to take stock of where you are and consider where you want to go. You may be a first-time leader feeling your way forward, an established leader who wants a reset, an experienced leader who wants to transform a culture, or that leader frantically trying to stay afloat after being tossed into the deep end of the corporate productivity pool.

No matter where you find yourself now, if your leadership dream has become a nightmare, now is the time for you to pause, make a plan, and begin your trek towards an InSPIRED Leadership summit. I've helped hundreds of leaders reach the summit, achieve their goals, and live a life that few experience. I've seen the lights come back on as the road ahead fills with invigorating adventure.

How do you get back to that adventure state? You lead intentionally. You make sure you have the adventure, rather than the adventure having you. If you've ever gone whitewater rafting, you know what I mean. When you're barreling down a raging river, and the raft starts to career, you feel an adrenaline rush. But that adrenaline only helps when you follow the guide. The guide has

> Life is too short to clock in, clock out, go home and do it all again the next day.

navigated that river a thousand times. He or she knows exactly when the bumps will hit, how hard they'll feel, how each rock affects the water's flow and raft, what to do with the paddles, how to integrate with other guides, and the critical ways to gain stability in the midst of chaos.

But when you are not intentional you're at the mercy of the water tossing your boat around the rapids and against the rocks.

As we engage in this InSPIRED leadership adventure together, allow me to come alongside as your guide. I've seen this process change individual leaders and turn entire companies around, multiplying productivity, profitability, and enjoyability.

Adventure is always, by definition, challenging, but the journey that follows will...

- Teach you to be intentional about how you lead.

- Help you serve others well.

- Reconnect you with your passion and the energy to do the things that matter to you.

- Equip you to integrate and work well with others to achieve great things.

- Empower you to be real and authentic, a leader people will gladly follow.

- Move you from theory to action as you execute on what you've learned.

- Help you develop a process to get where you want to go and reach your highest potential.

Perhaps most importantly, it will help you become a catalyst for creating an InSPIRED culture in your organization, your community, and beyond.

Life is too short to clock in, clock out, go home and do it all again the next day. Leadership is meant to be an exhilarating adventure as you answer the call to the summit. Whatever your summit may be, let's tackle it together.

TOOL KIT

Summary

- If your leadership dream has become a nightmare, let me give you some good news: it's not your fault if you were not set-up for success. But you are responsible for fixing it— Identifying your knowledge gaps, learning your unknowns, and developing a growth plan.

- Whether you are just starting your leadership journey or have been in leadership most of your career, one thing is always true: the leadership adventure can overwhelm.

- Uninspired leaders produce uninspired leadership.

- Imitation isn't just the sincerest form of flattery, it's also the quickest way to get results.

- Find awesome and copy it!

- An InSPIRED culture intentionally built by InSPIRED leaders produces an InSPIRED brand.

Action Steps

- **Check your inspiration levels.** Before you can even think about reaching your summit, you've got to reconnect with what inspires you. Take some time to think back and really delve into those sources of inspiration. Remind yourself why you were attracted to leadership in the first place.

- **Find awesome and copy it.** Think about who inspires you. Set up a time to talk with that person if possible and bring a list of questions. Make sure the questions are thoughtful and designed to help you become a better person and leader. Be respectful of their time and let them know you appreciate them.

- **Modify your systems.** Once you've done the research on what others do, you can apply what you've learned to your specific situation. Not everything will work for you, so pick what will and put it to work. When you start to see improvements be sure to let that person know how the advice helped you.

CHAPTER 3

INTENTIONAL

"That which occurs by chance is not an art."

—SENECA

Everest. The highest summit in the world can be a most unforgiving place. Mistakes at 28,000 feet can kill you and those you lead. Some people summit and get to experience the thrill of standing on top of the world. Most who are well prepared and lead well live to tell about it. But others never come back down the legendary mountain, even after enjoying their brief moment of triumph. More than 4,000 people have scaled the summit since Sir Edmund Hillary and Sherpa Tenzing Norgay first showed the way, but almost 300 have died trying to do so.

Leadership mistakes in the workplace may leave you breathing, but the damage can still be severe. So what separates leaders who succeed from those who mean well, but fail?

Looking to Everest may help answer that question. Many factors determine success or failure on Everest, but one story illustrates the single most critical leadership principle undergirding all others.

You may have seen the 2015 film *Everest* based on the true, but tragic, story of an attempted ascent in 1996 that left five climbers dead.

The film was based on a book by Beck Weathers, a climber who miraculously survived the ordeal. What the film, book, and popular accounts suggest is that the tragedy was primarily the result of a "freak," "rogue," and "unexpected" storm that caught climbers by surprise and led to several being stranded on the summit. However, of the many teams scheduled to ascend the summit at that time, only one proceeded under those conditions. In fact, one team associated with the National Geographic filming of the Everest IMAX documentary postponed their own ascent due to concerns about the weather. They lived to successfully scale the summit a few short days later. The teams that pressed past them did so in spite of warning signs both about the weather and their climbers' own fitness for the task.

Incredibly, in spite of the adverse conditions, twenty-three climbers made it to the summit of Everest on May 10. But the climbers led by veteran guides Rob Hall and Scott Fischer struggled up the mountain. They arrived late in the afternoon—a sign of trouble on Everest if ever there was one. If you recall from Chapter 2, if climbers had not begun their descent from the summit by 2 PM, the odds were against them making it back down before the deadly dark. When the predicted storm arrived around 4 PM that day, the descent path disappeared in whiteout conditions and hurricane-force winds. As a result, some climbers disappeared altogether. Others drifted off course and ended up stranded in the snow just a few hundred yards from camp.

One of those who drifted was author Beck Weathers. He was found, but left for dead after a brief examination. Incredibly, Weathers somehow staggered into camp the next day following a night on Everest face-down in the snow. He suffered severe frostbite and hypothermia, his right arm frozen solid. Somehow, with help from other climbers, he managed to survive and make his way lower down the mountain the next day, but with "the hands of a dead man." A helicopter barely managed to land in the rarefied air at a lower camp and transport him out.

On the initial descent from the summit, one climber collapsed in desperate need of oxygen. For reasons that remain unknown, guide Rob Hall chose to stay with the fallen climber and try to survive the night in what is commonly known as "the death zone" on Everest—anything above 23,000 feet. The climber likely died during the night, leaving Hall stranded with little energy and even less oxygen. At that altitude, the human brain functions at below half its normal capacity, affecting basic decision-making and motor skills. Eventually, after a grueling day and a half, Hall also succumbed to the cold, as the weather kept anyone from being able to rescue him in time. His guide partner Scott Fischer also died on the mountain that tragic day.

The *Everest* film, and even some accounts at the time, seemed to put all the blame for the deaths on the "freak" storm. However, one of Hall's clients, who did reach the summit that day and survived to tell his story in the book *Into Thin Air,* called the *Everest* movie version "total bull." Others who observed the horrific scene unfolding and engaged in rescue attempts that day concurred. The consensus among the other climbers was that the storm was not that unusual and that Everest climbers needed to be not only always aware but also respectful of rapidly changing conditions.

"People died because of their own personal decisions," said Lou Kasischke, who was climbing with Rob Hall. Just below the South Summit, when one of the climbing sherpas told him it was still two hours to the summit, Kasischke realized it was time to turn around. Two others on Hall's team also turned around near the South Summit, at 11:30 AM. The views around them were already blocked by clouds, and they sensed the weather was changing. "I didn't rescue anyone, and on summit day did nothing I can take pride in—except that at the critical moment I exercised the personal responsibility that each of us had and made a decision to turn around."

The fallen guides and clients had simply cut their safety margins too thin. One could say they drifted past the checkpoints that they themselves had set. Bottom line: they failed to be intentional.

A TALE OF TWO LEADERS

Rory and Bob were two visionary leaders with a strong drive to accomplish great things. Each wanted to be first-to-market in their shared industry. Each had identified a market objective that would put his organization on the map—but only if it achieved success first. The desire to achieve drove them to act when an opportunity presented itself.

When Rory heard of the opportunity, his start-up organization was already strong and well-prepared, although originally positioned to tackle a different objective. He chose to pivot to pursue this new opportunity. Because he had been intentional about building a first-rate team and resourcing them well, he was able to retool them quickly.

When Bob learned of Rory's new market focus, he became *reactionary*. He also decided to pivot and race for the objective, but he wasn't nearly as well prepared. His team wasn't as strong, nor was it resourced to deal with the inevitable struggles every team encounters when forging new ground. Bob's lack of intentional planning meant the resources and capital they did have were often squandered. Each failed opportunity lowered the morale of the organization. One by

> For every minute an athlete stands on the medal podium, there are years of disciplined activity.

one, his key performers lost interest and left to chase his or her own dreams. When what was left of Bob's team finally managed to achieve their objective—exhausted and frustrated—they had come in second place behind Rory's team. In that industry, second place might as well have been a total failure.

Rory's team had been prepared, strategic, and intentional. Bob's team had attempted to wing it and engage in a fire-drill-rush to market. Crushed after defeat, Bob had little left in his leadership tank and even less capital. His few remaining team members left him. His company never recovered and closed its doors permanently.

Maybe you've worked with a leader like Bob who rushed headlong into what looked like a golden opportunity, only to see it fail and leave everyone burned out and heading for the exits. You may even have been a leader like that and known the pain of seeing your summit dreams dashed. You may have survived, but barely, with painful scars to prove it.

For every moment of business acclaim, there must be countless hours of preparation. For every moment at the Everest summit, there are months of pre-planning. For every minute an athlete stands on the medal podium, there are years of disciplined activity. Success is never an accident. It always begins with being intentional, again and again.

Vince Lombardi is often credited with saying, "The man on the mountaintop didn't fall there." That's why being *Intentional* is the place to start if you want to achieve remarkable results as an InSPIRED leader.

If the story of Rory and Bob sounds familiar, you've probably heard it before. Rory? His real name was Roald Amundsen, the first person to reach the South Pole. Bob's real name was Robert Falcon Scott, the second person to reach the South Pole—five weeks later. By the time Scott arrived, he found a Norwegian flag and a note from "Rory."

Unfortunately for Scott and the other four members of his team, his failure to be intentional proved fatal. As a leader, you have a choice: be intentional on the front end—and multiply your chances of success. Or fail to do so—and multiply the pain of failure for you and the people you lead.

Unfortunately, for many leaders and organizations, *un*-intentionality is the norm. There may be a loose sketch of a plan or some grand vision, but little in terms of precisely how to get there. When leaders don't own the day, the day owns them—and their people pay the price.

I see it in organizations all the time. People act in constant fire-drill mode as management keeps them on high alert. Nerves fray, fuses get short, and relational explosions become a regular part of the workplace background noise. One person confided to me that the "always-on" environment felt like living with Post Traumatic Stress Disorder (PTSD) all the time.

> When leaders don't own the day, the day owns them—and their people pay the price.

Under this level of constant stress, productivity plummets, because it's hard for anyone to go too far in any one direction when pulled in twenty other directions. Why would someone take time to build any kind of efficiency when leadership will probably react to yet another shiny object tomorrow? Not to mention the impact this *un*-intentionality has on the quality of life outside of work.

So what happens? Talent always has a choice. The highly talented, high performers pack up and leave for a better place where intentional leadership, clear vision, and appreciation is the norm. Organizations are left with C and D players after the A-team bolts and the B-team slowly slips out the side exits. C and D players aren't particularly talented, but they've learned to survive within the chaos that *un-*intentionality brings. They do enough to stay out of the way, but not enough to make a positive contribution to the culture.

You may know what this feels like. Perhaps you've felt the pain before:

- **No prep.** You were promoted to a leadership role because you performed well at your current position. But no one equipped you. When you got here, you found landmines, silos, secret handshakes, and unwritten expectations. You shoulder the burden and do your best simply trying to stay one step ahead of the next crisis!

- **No path.** You have a job you enjoy at an organization you're proud to represent, but you want to advance. You know you are talented and create success for the organization, but there's no intentional advancement path for you. Leadership either doesn't know or doesn't care. You feel more like a cog in the machine than a critical part of the organization.

- **No clue.** You work under a leader who is clueless. He or she may project confidence, but it's untethered to reality. The team doesn't respect the leader, so there's an "every-man-for-himself, 8-in-the-gate, just-cash-the-check" mindset that permeates the team. You keep pushing forward but your efforts fall short without buy-in from everyone else.

- **No restraint.** You work for a leader or an organization whose appetite for achievement (and accompanying change) doesn't match the organization's metabolism or bandwidth. So everyone lives in a state of constant organizational indigestion—and all the potential ulcers that go with it.

It doesn't have to be this way! Imagine what your workplace would be like if intentionality were the norm rather than the exception. What if every employee was equipped and energized to bring their best to the table each day? What if people knew exactly where they fit and were provided the tools to contribute and thrive? What if leaders spent more time planning where to go and how to get there—and less time firefighting or looking over their shoulders at the competition?

Sound like an impossible dream? I assure you, it's not. Organizations like this do exist. In fact, as a leader, you can help your organization become a place like this.

EXCELLENCE IS NEVER AN ACCIDENT

It all begins with realizing that excellence is never an accident. It's always the result of being intentional. You have to have a plan. If you don't know where you're headed, you won't know how to prepare for the journey. When you're not savvy about the trail, you get caught up in the action of the day-to-day and forget to watch for checkpoints. When you're stuck in fire-ready-aim mode, you can easily drift off course.

That's why you must have an intentional plan to ensure you're hitting the right target consistently. So what sort of things must you be intentional about? Here are few to get started:

1. **Mindset.** Your mindset dictates everything else you do and everything you believe. If you aren't intentionally monitoring your mindset, you'll unintentionally believe things that will pull you off track.

2. **Yourself.** Being intentional about yourself means understanding who you are and who you are not. It's about having a plan to lead when strong and team when weak. It's being honest with yourself about who you are and who you hope to become.

3. **Your summit.** Not every summit is worth climbing, so be intentional about choosing yours. Once you know where you want and need to go, you can get intentional about making the climb.

4. **Your team.** Provide good leadership for them, because they are a critical component of the climb. Good leadership is an art, and, as Seneca put it, "That which occurs by chance is not an art."

5. **Your culture.** Good culture empowers your team and kickstarts execution. Culture eats strategy for breakfast.

6. **Operations.** Be intentional about what you need to deliver. Then create a solid plan to get it done.

7. **Your organizational structure and goals.** Do you do business by design or by accident?

8. **Your customers.** At the end of the day, they will determine your success or failure.

THE DESTINY MINDSET

Have you ever been driving to a place you've never been before and become disoriented? Maybe you turned left when you should have gone right, or you zoomed past your exit because you were talking. How likely is it that you'll end up at your destination without at least pausing to take stock of where you are and implementing a plan to get where you need to go? Not likely.

The same principle holds true in leadership. When you find yourself off course, you must make course corrections. Accidental successes are neither repeatable nor sustainable. That's why you must lead to succeed on purpose. Think about the ballerina who stands for hours *en pointe,* wooden blocks digging bloody gashes into her toes, so she can hop to her toes effortlessly and glide across the stage when the curtain goes up. Those graceful movements don't happen by accident. She practices for decades to perform with excellence in that moment.

If you prefer an example with more speed, think about the painstaking years that go into engineering a Formula One race car. An entire team of experts meticulously designs every aspect of the vehicle for maximum speed and aerodynamics to achieve a single purpose— to win the checkered flag. Likewise, no mountaineer ever reached the summit accidentally. Careful planning, intentional preparation, and a firm understanding of your destination position you to reach whatever your own summits may be.

All of it makes up what I call the Destiny Mindset. As you may notice, the words *destiny*[5] and *destination*[6] share the same root— *destinare,* which is Latin for "make firm, establish." While the word *destiny* carries the idea of being "predetermined and sure to come true," your *destination* is something you "determine, appoint, choose, make firm or fast." Unless you predetermine your destiny, you'll never reach your destination, let alone make the moves required to get there.

> I believe each of us is destined for greatness.

Without intentionality, you'll be the disoriented driver cruising down the road, always in motion, but clueless about which way to turn. Sure, you'll get somewhere, but will it be the destiny you long to fulfill? I challenge you to refuse to operate in this haphazard way. Don't mistakenly equate movement with momentum or action with results.

Too many good people simply accept whatever happens as their lot in life. However, when you adopt a Destiny Mindset, you plant your flag and proclaim to yourself and the world: *I believe I have a higher purpose. That purpose is my chosen destination.* I believe each of us is destined for greatness. Visualize the destiny you want, then develop an intentional plan to reach that destination.

CONVERT THOUGHTS INTO ACTIONS

A Destiny Mindset will get you nowhere unless you take action. To choose the right actions, you must know your context: determine where you are headed, the moves that will get you there, and what it will take to ready your organization to achieve it. Although we leaders are always in the people business, you must make the moves. If you are going to achieve your destiny as a leader, you've got to dream big, gain clarity, and then put success systems into place to achieve remarkable results. These intentional processes will ultimately allow you to be able to scale on purpose.

Start with this basic framework to help you think about how best to develop a process for systematic improvement. Remember to be intentional with:

- **You.** Success starts with being clear on your own personal destination. As I mentioned, if you know where you want to end up, you can put processes and systems in place to ensure you get there.

- **Internal Customers.** Put processes into place that equip your team, your peers, or (if you are an owner, CEO, or C-Suite leader) your entire organization . Each person in your company needs clarity on the destination and an intentional process to get there. Because they look to you for direction, you must provide them with an environment and systems in which they can, in fact, achieve the destination.

- **External Customers.** Your customers, shareholders, and other stakeholders are ultimately the ones who benefit most when you get intentional about growth and performance. The clarity and focus of your systems empower your team to deliver predictably superior service that results in satisfied customers—and a healthy bottom line.

This framework—you, internal customers, external customers—lays the foundation for maximum optimization. From there, if you have any hope of reaching your destination and seeing the summit, then you must become intentional with your systems and processes. Identify the ideal or optimal. Start with you, then work outward. Forget about the journey of a thousand miles. Take the steps. Invest the time to get clear on your destination, then develop a plan to reach it—and then take the next best step. If you intentionally work the system and diligently engage the process, you *can* reach your destination.

> Dream big. Gain clarity. Create success systems.

WHAT'S YOUR DITLO?

As a leader, you will develop a reputation based on your activity—what you do over time. Your reputation with your internal customers or team and your reputation as an organization will develop the same way. How others experience you as a leader over time becomes your leadership brand. You are the sum of all your parts—strengths, weaknesses, successes, failures, highs, and lows. Every move you make (or don't make) influences your brand.

That's why you've got to be intentional with your actions. Your moves determine how others experience you and how they expect you to act. If you've been ill-prepared, erratic, and arbitrary in your leadership, both your team and your organization already know it, even if no one has the courage to tell you. If you were an expedition guide taking a team to summit Everest, no one would want to go with you. But if you are intentional and considerate, people will follow you.

If your reputation is based on what you do, then it makes sense to pay attention to what you do on a daily basis. Your habits will make or break your team. The key difference between InSPIRED leaders and everyone else is that InSPIRED leaders use the power of intentional habits in day-to-day leadership. When excellence becomes a habit, you begin to separate from the rest of the pack. Amateurs practice until they get it right. Professionals practice until they can't get it wrong.

Success happens in what I call the DITLO, or day-in-the-life-of *you*. What happens in the DITLO determines your success, but it doesn't start all at once. It begins with seemingly small, incremental changes that compound over time. When you intentionally implement daily habits, you don't have to worry about ten years from now, or even next year. You focus on doing the right things today and work the process to reach the summit.

Most mountaineers who died on Everest, for example, didn't fall from the mountain. They simply stopped putting one foot in front of the other and froze to death. As Bill Gates put it, "People overestimate what can be done in two years, and they underestimate the power of what can be done in ten." Zig Ziglar put it this way: "Hurricanes and earthquakes get all the press, but termites do more damage and they take such little bitty bites!" Small actions, intentionally repeated daily, will ultimately determine your success.

If it's true that you make your habits, and then your habits make you, what habits should you intentionally put in place? Ask yourself: Is there a model of best practice habits I could imitate? The trick is to benchmark the best and replicate for results. Remember: find awesome and copy it! Find someone whose process worked exceptionally well. Discover their habits, and do what they do. There's no need to reinvent the wheel.

Think back on the people who have inspired you. What were their characteristics and competencies? If you paused to think about them in the previous chapter, think about the habits of those people you listed. What's the simplest way for you to start implementing those habits and behaviors in your own life and leadership?

I believe you can get anywhere you want in life by taking small, daily steps in the right direction. If you want to make 10,000 widgets a day, the likely starting point is not at 10,000 widgets a day. Can you make 50? Then 100? Then 500? 1000? When you intentionally improve in small increments, you build muscle memory and strengthen those DITLO processes and habits. Ultimately, those habits, both personally and organizationally, will take you where you want to go.

> Amateurs practice until they get it right. Professionals practice until they can't get it wrong.

Be intentional about your destination, but don't neglect what you need to do each day. You climb Everest one step at a time, at the right time of year, with the right timing, and with wise guides. Your own InSPIRED leadership adventure also

happens one intentional step at a time, with wise guides and sound processes. You may be able to do it once, but can you do it over and over again? Is your success repeatable, sustainable, and scalable? Are you building the professional muscle
memory so that you can't get it wrong
because it is so ingrained in you and
your organization?

Discover the habits you need and build those microbehaviors into your organization. They will lead you to key performance indicators that determine whether you are on the right track. They become the performance checkpoints that determine if you're making your way to the summit or drifting off course.

KNOW THE TOPOGRAPHY

Most people prefer to remain blissfully ignorant, thinking that what they don't know they can't be blamed for. But that's an uninspired way of thinking and doesn't work. Once you know your destination and understand what habits are key to success, you need to get intentional about one more thing—your organizational topography.

Think of it as the context for your journey. You can't get where you want to go if you are unaware of the obstacles you'll face along the way. The best-laid plans always meet resistance when put into practice. That's why it is incumbent on leaders to discover both the knowns and the unknowns. It begins with taking stock of where you are as a leader, where your team is in relation to the goal, and where the organization is in relation to its goals.

Knowing the organizational topography simply means getting the lay of the land. If you were at Everest base camp getting acclimated to the altitude, you wouldn't simply sit around waiting to execute on your phenomenal plan to reach your destination. You'd be doing your homework, examining ice fields and mapping ways across, evaluating your equipment, and getting to know your guides. Such detail work makes sure your plan has the best chance of success. Studying topography requires patience and forward-thinking vision, which is why so few leaders take the time to do it. But you can't understand what you'll encounter on the journey if you aren't intentional about studying the terrain first.

A major component of organizational topography is understanding how your organization defines a leader. Leadership definitions distinguish your organization from any other organization. They show what your company culture values as opposed to other cultures. For example, North American-centric organizations tend to value action. Other cultures tend to value planning. So if you tend to take action, you'll be perceived as a leader in most American organizations, but in another country, you might be perceived as impetuous. The topography matters. If you don't take the time to learn it, you'll get it wrong despite your best efforts.

You've got to be intentional, but you've got to be intentional based on the conditions that exist where you are. What does your leader value? What does your organization value? Just like the topography of Everest dictates that there are only certain possible routes to the summit, your organizational topography will dictate the way you can get to where you need to go. Once you know the topography, you can move forward intentionally.

LEADER: IT'S UP TO YOU

When you become intentional as a leader, two things happen. First, you establish your authority—not in positional power, but as someone to be respected. Without wise leadership, you'll quickly lose the respect and trust of your team. Intentionality sets you apart as a leader worth following because it proves you have a big picture vision (think "high beam" headlights) as well as day-to-day savvy (think "low beam" lights). Remember, small habits executed daily over time produce remarkable results.

Second, when you are intentional, you establish authenticity. You give other people clarity on who you are and how you lead. Plus, your team or organization will value your earnest attempts to get off the fire-drill treadmill so you can grow together at scale and speed—without everyone becoming zombies.

Teams will follow you as they see you consider all factors, make a plan, evaluate your organizational topography, and live out your leadership in the DITLO. You won't always be perfect, and you will make mistakes, but even in those times, being intentional will position you to be authentic.

TOOL KIT

Summary

- For every minute an athlete stands on the medal podium, there are years of disciplined activity.

- When leaders don't own the day, the day owns them—and their people pay the price.

- Talent always has a choice.

- Excellence is never an accident. It always begins with being intentional.

- Dream big. Gain clarity. Create success systems.

- Scale your success systems: Repeatable, Sustainable, Scalable

- Amateurs practice until they get it right. Professionals practice until they can't get it wrong.

- Learn how to succeed in your Organizational Topography.

Action Steps

- **Own your day.** Who is in charge of your day? Is it you or someone else? Your most limiting resource is time. Keep track of how you spend your time in 30-minute increments. Then, after a week or two, review where your time is spent and make adjustments so your day belongs to you.

- **Map your trail.** If you don't know where you are going, how will you ever know if you get there? Take some time to discover where you are, where you want to go, and the routes you must take to get there. This exercise can be used as your InSPIRED Leadership trail guide.

- **Know your DITLO.** Finding awesome and copying it means doing the things that awesome people do daily. Get intentional about where you want to go, and then find someone who is already there. Study their habits and shortcuts so you can apply them to your life and leadership.

- **Know your organization.** Knowing what leadership means to your leader and to your organization is critical. What does your organization value? What gets regarded? What gets rewarded? How do the most effective team members achieve results in THIS organization? Learn to be organizationally savvy.

CHAPTER 4

SERVICE

"To give real service you must add something which cannot be bought or measured with money, and that is sincerity and integrity."

—DOUGLAS ADAMS

A uthor and leadership expert Ken Blanchard tells a story about a particularly poor customer service experience. He and his wife had separated while shopping at the mall. At one point, Ken had found some clothes he wanted to try on, but he wanted his wife's opinion before purchasing. The only problem was that he had no phone to call her. Ken asked the clerk at the counter if he could use the store phone to call his wife before making the purchase. The salesperson replied, "They don't even let us use the phone here. Why would I let you?"

Ken promptly placed the clothing back on the rack, thanked the gentleman for his time, and walked out of the store. He never went back. No doubt the store leadership had a good reason for not letting employees talk on the phone, likely so they would focus on customers right in front of them. But the *way* leadership enforced that policy translated into the way the clerk treated Ken the customer—the very opposite of the reason the policy was created in the first place.

Here's the lesson for you as an InSPIRED leader. Modeled behavior transfers and permeates throughout the organization. You can have the best and most intentional plans to achieve results, but if you aren't intentional about excellent customer service, you'll lose every time.

Everyone in business knows this, and you're probably thinking, *I would never treat a customer that way!* But what about how you serve those you lead? We serve others by enrolling, influencing, and connecting with them. How you serve the people you lead in your own team or organization is ultimately how they will serve—or not serve—your customers. A service mindset is critical both inside and outside of your organization, to your

> Modeled behavior transfers and permeates throughout the organization.

internal customers as well as your external customers. For example, how you enforce rules internally can determine how you and your organization are perceived externally.

Are you service-oriented or transactional? Do you enforce the letter of the law or the spirit of the law? Is your brand known for serving others or serving the company? Service or self-centeredness? Those answers will go a long way toward creating a brand perception of you and your team or organization.

In the entertainment industry, the Emmy Awards go to the best television performances and the Oscars for excellence in film. But there is another award given every year—the Razzies. While the Emmys and Oscars go to the best, the Razzies go to the worst. As you reflect on your own customer service experiences, you can probably recall businesses worthy of a Razzie for poor service.

But what award would your customers give you? What about members of your team? What award would they give you for how well you lead them? It's critical to put yourself in the shoes and the mind of your customer and evaluate what they experience. It's the only way to catch service drift and get back on track. Do you deserve an Emmy or a Razzie? If you don't know, you'd better find out quickly. Here's why.

The customer is the reason you are in business. At the end of the day, if you don't serve your customers, both external and internal, you won't be in business for long. Kenneth B. Elliott, Vice President in Charge of Sales for the Studebaker Corporation, once defined the key place of service by defining what a customer is not:

> There are several common denominators to be found when we consider the customer in terms of what he is not. These things, I think, are fundamental to intelligent customer relationship and, it may be added, most of them apply pretty well to the vast majority of prospects as well.

1. The customer is not dependent upon us—we are dependent upon him.

2. The customer is not an interruption of our work—he is the purpose of it.

3. The customer is not a rank outsider to our business—he is a part of it.

4. The customer is not a statistic—he is a flesh-and-blood human being completely equipped with biases, prejudices, emotions, pulse, blood chemistry and possibly a deficiency of certain vitamins.

5. The customer is not someone to argue with or match wits against—he is a person who brings us his wants. If we have sufficient imagination we will endeavor to handle them profitably to him and to ourselves.

The point is this: customers are not a nuisance to be managed, but the very reason you lead. We're all somebody's customer. The customer may not always be right, but the customer must always be served. Take care of and serve your customers with respect, and they'll reward you with loyalty, consistency, and profitability. When you serve with excellence, you reinforce or establish your brand and create momentum. Conversely, when you serve poorly, or not at all, you diminish your brand. Even worse, you put a bad taste in the mouth of the very people you rely on to succeed.

THE HIGH COST OF POOR SERVICE

Once when I was in a jewelry store, I watched an attempt at service go awry—and take the customer with it. I was looking at jewelry with the help of a saleswoman when a couple walked in the door. I noted that their skin color was darker and that the woman wore a bindi on her forehead indicating her Hindu faith and, likely, Indian descent.

In an attempt to give prompt service and acknowledge the couple, the saleswoman eagerly turned to them and called out, "Uno momento, por favor!" in broken Spanish. I cringed as the stunned and offended customers left the store. I myself searched for the fastest exit from the awkward situation. It's one thing to want to serve, but you have to serve accurately.

> The customer may not always be right, but the customer must always be served.

Being customer-centric means being aware enough to know how other people experience you, because a poor service experience can cost a lot. When I first started in sales, we talked about the nine-to-one ratio. It took nine positive experiences to overcome one negative experience. A customer who had a bad experience would tell nine friends, but only share the details of a good experience once.

That was then. Thanks to social media, your disgruntled customer can tweet, post, or share the experience to 900, 9,000, or even 9 million people in an instant. The stakes have been raised in the service game.

The problem is the disconnect between company and customer. According to *The Customer Experience Index* study released by Forrester, 80% of organizations believe they're delivering superior customer service. But how many customers believe they're experiencing superior customer service? *Only 8%!* What we have here is a failure to communicate. Either companies don't know what good customer service is, they don't care, or they aren't trying to speak their customer's language. The study made this startling observation:

> Roughly 63% of companies simply have no clue what their customers want. They are drowning in assumptions about what their company's customer service experience is like with no real knowledge of their customer's expectations.[7]

Ouch. According to *Entrepreneur Magazine*, poor customer service costs US businesses an average of $83 billion in lost revenue every year.[8] The list of things that drives customers crazy includes deception, rudeness, incompetency, inflexibility, and lateness. You would think those things should be easy to address if the customer is truly valued.

Another sobering statistic: it costs five times as much to acquire new customers as it does to keep those you already have. So if the data proves that poor customer service is a huge drain on your bottom line, how do you make sure you aren't dealing a fatal wound with your service? It starts with a change of heart.

DO YOU HAVE THE HEART TO SERVE?

Much of what it takes to become an InSPIRED leader in the area of service starts with your heart. Just like a climber scaling Everest, if you lose sight of the passion that drove you to start the adventure, all of your other preparations will likely fall short when the going gets tough. On the mountain, not caring can cost you your life.

In business, it can cost your livelihood. You can put all the processes in place to serve customers, but if you don't have the *heart to serve*, people will see it. Service becomes something you do to the customer because you have to, rather than something you do *for* the customer because you want to. Forced customer service feels hollow because it *is* hollow.

Serving customers with your heart begins with better understanding them in your head. Where are they coming from? What needs do they have? You have to know them inside and out, backward and forwards to know what they really want. Only then can you serve them well. You can be as accommodating as possible, but if you aren't meeting their exact needs, they'll look for someone who can. The way to do this? *Ask.* When you build a relationship with your customers, you earn the right to ask questions. Those questions help you get to the heart of their needs.

Once you know the needs, you can move towards how you will meet those needs experientially with a serving heart. Then you can go beyond the transaction and deliverable to deepen the relationship. What people want is often something drastically different than what you think. Once you discover it, you can craft an intentional plan to wow them with service you know exceeds their expectations. The goal is always to deliver an amazing experience that blows them away.

If you simply look for transactions, you may find sales, but you'll always feel the pressure to find the next one. Instead, focus on getting to know the potential customer so you can do an accurate diagnostic. Prescribing a solution without a diagnosis is malpractice. It's better to build partnerships based on providing incredible service that meets the true needs and keeps them coming back for more.

YOUR INVERTED ORG CHART

Many organizations think they can simply dictate what good service means. But that's not the way it works. The customer experience should *always* be the North Star defining good service.

When you make a customer-first approach the foundation of your business, it changes the entire organization. I think of it as an inverted organizational chart. You're probably familiar with a typical org chart. It's a pyramid with the leader at the top, then the VPs, middle managers, supervisors, employees, and finally—at the very bottom, or maybe even outside the pyramid—is the customer.

But in the inverted org chart, the North Star is the customer. The customer sits above an inverted pyramid. And the people with frontline interaction, the ones who were at the bottom before, are now at the top and make up the widest part of the organization. That's where superior service begins. Frontline employees become preeminent because they are the first point of contact for the customer. They control what customers experience when they interact with the organization.

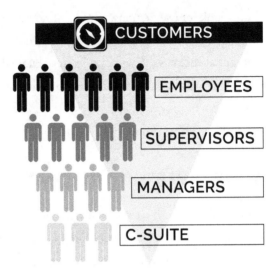

Based on this inverted org chart model:

- **The front line becomes preeminent.** They are the internal customers who most directly serve external customers. Equip them, and give them the authority, to serve well.

- **Supervisors serve the front line** who serves the **customers.**

- **Managers serve the supervisors** who serve the front line who serves the **customers.**

- **The executive team serves the managers** who serve the supervisors who serve the front line who serve the **customers.**

When you invert the org chart to focus on serving customers, you essentially change every person's job description from a privilege to an opportunity. In essence, you begin to change the culture of your organization by creating InSPIRED leaders from the bottom up (or top down, depending on your perspective).

ARCHITECT THE SYSTEMS TO SUPPORT THE HEART

If focusing on service is a significant step on the InSPIRED leadership path, how do you go about making superior service an everyday practice? You guessed it—by being *Intentional.* Great service doesn't happen by accident. Every member of your organization is a person who has good days and bad days. Without a detailed plan in place for excellent customer service, you'll only get the best any of those people can bring themselves to give on any given day. But if you architect superior service every step of the way, you'll know in advance, and with great certainty, what customers will experience. You'll be able to deliver the gold standard when you define what optimal service must look like for your customer.

As I serve business leaders and organizations around the world, I travel quite a bit and stay in many hotels. Sometimes my wife goes with me. When we visit San Diego, my wife loves to stay at the Hotel del Coronado (or Hotel Del). If you've never experienced the Hotel Del, it is a magical place to stay. It was built in 1888 and turned into a National Historic Landmark in 1977. It has hosted presidents, movie stars, and all manner of famous people. Located right on the Pacific Ocean and just outside downtown San Diego, it has a unique vibe.

When we visited a few years ago, we checked in, got our keys, and went to the room. When we opened the door, the room looked nice, but no different than any other hotel room. Plus, it faced the parking lot, so the view wasn't great. A little disappointed, I went back down to the front desk clerk and explained that I was here with my wife and needed a bit of downtime. I asked if she might be able to put us in a better room.

Her response was InSPIRED customer service in action. She clicked a few keys on her computer, issued new room keys, and sent us to the new room. We walked down the hall both nervous and excited to see what was behind the next door.

As we swung open the door, the view took our breath away. This Californian cabana looked out over beautiful landscape and onto the Pacific Ocean. Out the back door was a small patch of grass that transitioned to the dunes and then on to the beach. An incredible beach vibe immediately washed over us as we felt the stress slip away. We could hear waves crashing with immense power and beauty. Sunlight streamed in through windows and doors, as the salty smell of the ocean permeated everything. It was the polar opposite of the parking lot view in the other room.

Did the lady at the front desk have to upgrade us to this room? Certainly not. But in doing so, she delivered a *wow* experience like nothing I've ever experienced. That was no accident. Long before we arrived, someone architected that experience, empowering and encouraging her as a frontline employee to make superior customer service a top priority. No matter your industry, when you deliver that kind of experience to your customers, you set yourself apart from your competitors. Any hotel could provide us with a decent room and a continental breakfast, but Hotel Del provided us with an experience we're still talking about. Even better, we committed this year to annual stays by joining Hotel Del's Club level membership. After this particularly outstanding teammate served us well, we more than returned the value of her service.

Make this level of service part of your value proposition. Anyone can do what you can do, but no one can do it the way you do it. I call it serving others "from tip to tail." It means you see customers as valued individuals, without whom you wouldn't exist. Architect a *wow* experience to make service your strength. Lean into it—and shine.

SERVICE IS AN EMOTIONAL EXPERIENCE

Did you know that over 70% of buying experiences are based on how customers *feel* they are being treated? Seven out of ten Americans say they are willing to spend more with companies they believe provide excellent service and with whom they *feel* connected. One study reported that 86% of consumers in the US said they stopped doing business with a company because of a bad client experience. Of this percentage, 55% cited a company's failure to resolve their problems in a timely manner.[9]

There's no getting around it. Service—either good or bad—is an emotional experience. Your customer contracts with you in the hope that you can fulfill your promise, but hope deferred is problematic. Anytime you sell something, you create an expectation in somebody's mind. For that reason, you have to be intentional about the emotional experience that follows. And this emotional management piece is where most people and organizations fall short. They hook the customer with the intention of meeting customer needs but give little thought to the comprehensive customer experience. But if 70% of a customer's decision to purchase (or purchase again) is based on how the customer feels, you'd better have a plan in place to manage their emotional experience.

If you're wired to be more rational and find yourself resisting all this talk of emotion, I get it. But consider this: emotion fires before reason in the human brain, even for logical thinkers. When you deliver good or bad service, an emotion fires in the customer's brain before a thought. Often that emotion will trump whatever thoughts may follow. If seven out of ten customers are willing to spend more money with companies and organizations they feel connected to, then InSPIRED leaders must capitalize on that reality.

By the way, this emotional awareness doesn't only apply to external customers, but to internal customers, as well. Seven out of ten of your peers, coworkers, direct reports, and colleagues are willing to buy what you are selling, if—and this is a big if—they feel emotionally connected with you. That means you must give them respect and serve them well, too.

I encourage you to start evaluating your service experience with two questions: First, how healthy is service *inside* your organization right now? If you find morale is low, it could be that your level of service is the reason. Rather than reflexively blame your team members, consider these tips to serve them well:

- Don't saturate them with change.

- Use effective change management.

- Provide effective project management.

- Plan and communicate those plans.

- Be consistent in attitude and action.

- Listen to your direct reports who are probably closer to the customer needs.

- Care for your team rather than insist they sprint endlessly.

Second, how healthy is your team service to those *outside* your organization? Of course, your customers will let you know if you aren't serving them well. But you may need to be intentional about asking them before it's too late. Remember, there is a significant gap between the level of service most companies think they deliver and what customers think they receive. Pay attention to what your customers tell you and use their feedback to architect a better, more intentional experience on an ongoing basis.

Third, as an individual leader, where is your level of service to others right now? It's one thing to serve well organizationally, but every organization is made up of individuals, and you are one of those individuals. This means you need to constantly check your own service level and commit to making continual improvements. How your external customers experience you and how your internal customers react to you will tell the story of your service and define your personal leadership brand.

WHAT TO DO WHEN YOU FAIL TO WOW

No matter how focused you are on customers, sometimes things don't go according to plan. You or your team will slip up and let a customer down. You can't be perfect all the time, but you can be honest.

I pride myself on delivering superior service, but I once made a major error and had to work hard to fix it. I showed up at a training event forty-five minutes early. As I was going over my notes to prepare for the day, my phone started blowing up. It was the customer—texting and calling like crazy. Then it hit me: I hadn't taken the time zone difference into account when I put the event on my calendar. I wasn't forty-five minutes early—I was fifteen minutes late!

Ugh. That sinking feeling in my gut was not good. Here I am, the InSPIRED leadership guy, about to deliver a talk about delivering superior service to a room full of people who expected me to start a teaming session fifteen minutes ago. I dashed to the venue, owned up to my mistake, and managed to still wrap up on time.

After the event, I knew I had to recover with this client for two reasons. First, I knew how I reacted would say a lot about my brand. If I did it right, I could increase my standing with this client. If not,

I could end what had been a positive relationship. I came up with a recovery plan and let the client decide on the best remedy.

I offered either not to charge them for the day of training I had just delivered or to come back to do an additional day of training at no charge. The offer affirmed how much I valued the relationship with them and prompted an understanding reply. The client told me they didn't want me to make a special trip, but when I was back in town they would like for me to come back by for another event. So that's exactly what happened. I did a half-day workshop, which is what they wanted, to make up for my mistake. I let them choose the best recovery option that would serve their needs.

But as Paul Harvey used to say, here's the rest of the story. The client with whom I had made the mistake recommended me to her boss. As a result, I did an event for her boss, as well. The intentional response to my mistake led to more business. Showing up fifteen minutes late could have sealed my fate with that organization. Instead of a recommendation to her boss, it could have turned into a tarnished reputation for me in the industry. My recovery plan cost me some time and money, but in the long run, I gained it back on the next event.

More importantly, I relearned a valuable lesson in customer service. Mistakes are going to happen, so you need to plan to recover from them. Mistakes can actually bond you better, further, and faster to a customer, because a relationship isn't truly known and trusted until it fails and is repaired.

When intentionally designing your customer experience, be sure to build in a recovery plan. Let customers know what will happen when things don't go perfectly (because they know nothing ever does). Even the best plans need adjusting from time to time. It also reassures them to know that you have a plan for recovery even before you start to build the relationship.

Consequently, when I consult with organizations, I have them give their recovery plan a name like The Client Optimization Program. This trips a psychological switch in the customer's mind that you have a plan for recovery should it ever be needed. It assures them that they're working with a professional who is honest about the

> Leaders have the right to boss, but a responsibility to serve.

potential problems and comes prepared with a plan to fix them and get to a better state.

Do this well, and when the inevitable problems arise, they won't panic. They'll trust you to deliver upon your promise and *wow* them with your service.

LEADERS: SERVICE BEGINS WITH YOU

Leaders have the right to boss, but a responsibility to serve. In the inverted org chart, who is at the bottom of the upside-down pyramid? The highest positional leader in the organization. So what do you think will happen if that leader doesn't model superior service? The entire pyramid will topple under its own unsustainable weight.

That's why service begins with leaders like you. You have to take ownership of how you serve your internal stakeholders so you can influence how they take ownership of the customer experience. It starts by asking yourself some key questions:

- **How often do you think of the people you lead as being there for you?** The way you treat your people will determine how they treat the customer. Don't take that for granted.

- **Are you more of a coach or a correctional officer?** Coaches bring out the best in their people for a team win. Correctional officers make individuals cower and do "just enough" to not get singled out.

- **How well do you intentionally build amazing team synergy?** Great teams that work together to win have synergy where each person serves the others and brings out the best in others. Synergy compounds results and leads to victory.

- **Are you here to equip, empower, delineate, delegate, and expand, or are you here to be served so you can advance?** Great leaders put their people in a position to win, and in doing so, they share in the victories.

- **How well do new employees experience your culture as service-oriented?** People form instant opinions of your leadership skills and style. How they experience you from the start influences how effective they'll be in the future and how well they'll serve each other and the customer. What are the first fifteen minutes like with you? The first six to twelve weeks? Good leaders instantly make their people feel like part of the team, not a newbie that has to earn their stripes.

Do you have this attitude toward service on your team or in your organization? If not, you have a heart problem, not a hand problem.

> Great leaders put their people in a position to win, and in doing so, they share in the victories.

The hands can't fully operationalize what the heart doesn't believe. If you are a service-and-support-oriented leader, you are in a unique position to unleash the power of your team. Many people confuse a servant leader with a weak leader. They think that in serving your team, you give all your power away. Nothing could be further from the truth. Teams will lay down their lives for servant leaders. A servant leader can be a gritty leader but serve with others in mind.

You can't demand discretionary effort. It has to be given. You can never self-declare as the leader of your team. You can declare yourself to be a manager or supervisor, but *leader* is a term of endearment given by the team based on your level of connectedness. A great leader touches the heart first, and the hands follow. If you go for the hands first, if you try to get compliance, you may not get it. But if you go for the heart, by inspiring and serving your team, they'll give you everything you need and more.

So let me challenge you to be a servant leader, regardless of your position or title. See the needs of the team and organization. Then equip, empower, delineate, delegate, and serve your team. I assure you, remarkable results will follow, and you will be on your way to becoming an InSPIRED leader worth following.

TOOL KIT

Summary

- Modeled behavior transfers and permeates the entire organization.

- A service mindset is critical both *inside* and *outside* of your organization.

- It's critical to consider how others experience you because a bad experience comes at a high cost.

- When you've built a relationship with your customers, you've earned the right to ask questions. Those questions help you get to the heart of their needs.

- When you're intentionally designing your customer experience, be sure to build in a recovery plan.

Startling Statistics

- 80% of organizations believe they deliver superior service. But *only 8%* of customers believe they receive superior service.

- It takes nine positive experiences to overcome one negative experience. So any customer who has a bad experience will relate that story *nine times* to the people they know. They may only share the details of a good experience once.

- 70% of buying experiences are based on how customers *feel* they are treated.

Action Steps

- **Perform a customer service audit.** Is serving your customers something you *do* or is it who you *are*? Apply this to both internal and external customers. Which areas of the customer service experience deliver less than a WOW experience? Put yourself in your customer's shoes. What would you want that isn't being delivered?

- **Invert your org chart.** Think about all of the people who are on the front lines of customer service. How could you serve them better so they could serve others? Ask them what they need to do their job better and see how you can make that happen.

- **Define a *wow* experience.** Think about your customers, both internal and external. Come up with a list of actions to deliver an experience that blows them away and exceeds their wildest expectations.

CHAPTER 5

PASSION

*"What lies behind us and what lies before us
are tiny matters compared to what lies within us."*
—RALPH WALDO EMERSON

When I first started helping to scale the construction company I told you about earlier, I enjoyed tremendous success. The company's annual revenue ran right around $600,000 per year at first, but the potential for growth was high. I worked diligently to implement systems and processes to maximize growth.

I began by focusing on sales, tapping into emerging marketplace opportunities. I did a competitor analysis to see where we stacked up. I streamlined the sales processes with internal systems. I worked on professional marketing materials and made sure we had a sales support system to scale with our growth.

When we overran our production capacity and had a four- to six-month backlog, I began investigating internal ways to fix our infrastructure. I started with the accounting system because you can't measure what you don't track. It quickly became apparent that we would need new financing options and new systems for working with customer deposits and collectibles. After we revamped that process, I moved into the production side to develop processes and checklists that ensured quality control.

That year we managed to grow the business to almost $3 million in revenue on Herculean effort! We produced 400% growth while building out the infrastructure. The underlying process had been tweaked, but most of the time we were operating as a $1 million business trying to throughput $3 million in revenue. We just kept growing and revising our systems. One key value propelled us: regardless of internal struggles, we took care of the customer—100%!

Unfortunately, that job trained me to isolate my passion. I had become quite good in the construction niche. I understood workflow and discovered the keys to unleashing the best in the workforce. I learned the best methods to get us operating efficiently at speed and scale. I thrived on the challenge and loved being the fixer, the guy that made the magic happen. But I wasn't passionate about constructing buildings, per se. I was passionate about people, leadership, strategy, and business. Empowering people to succeed lit me up and got me excited in a way that nothing else did. I felt sure that by using my strengths of quick thinking and strategic insight, I could become a force multiplier for success and serve people in a way that both benefited them and rewarded me.

So I had to make a decision. I could have made an excellent living consulting with and running construction companies. But after experiencing that level of burnout, I leaned into aligning my work with my passion and higher purpose. I decided to step out of the safe zone and take a risk. Because I had managed a bit of a financial safety net, I decided to jump and make my passion my business.

It used to be that passion didn't rank high on the priority list when people were looking for a job, but that has been changing rapidly. Think about your first job and why it became your first job.

Maybe it was the only place in town that was hiring, or perhaps you had a connection through a relative. Maybe a friend or family member hired you and gave you a chance to put something on your resume. In other words, if you're like most people, your entry into the job market probably wasn't all that intentional.

In fact, in the history of the working world, passion seldom came into the conversation about making a living. Before the Industrial Revolution, the focus was on survival and providing for basic needs. As people moved out of the country and into the city, they began to specialize. Entire cities became known for housing specific industries as generations of workers did one kind of job depending on where they lived. Passion never entered the equation.

In the second half of the Twentieth Century, however, prosperity in the Western world began to change people's definition of work. There was still a focus on skilled trades, but as the century progressed, workers began pursuing careers that interested them instead of resigning themselves to doing what their parents did. Higher education, easier transportation, and technological advances increased the income potential and options for children of Baby Boomers.

Today, the place of passion in the workforce is still in a state of flux. Millennials get a bad rap for their work ethic and propensity to bounce from job to job. But it's not that they won't work long and hard. They just won't unlock that drive unless it's for something that matters and makes an impact. They realize the value of pursuing a meaningful job, not just one that pays the bills.

This transition from work as a way to provide for yourself and your family to work as a means of making a difference in the world now shapes the modern workplace. Leaders ignore it at their own peril. Leaders must consider the place of passion in their organizational culture and leadership styles. If they don't, they will struggle to attract and retain top talent and to achieve remarkable results. In today's world—more than ever—passion determines production.

GOIN' THROUGH THE MOTIONS

Everyone can relate to doing a job they don't enjoy. It's natural to look with longing at what we think is the next great thing on the horizon. According to Gallup research, "An astounding *70 percent* of U.S. employees are not showing up to work fully committed to delivering their best performance. Adding insult to injury, 52 percent of those workers are basically sleepwalking through their day, and 18 percent of them are busy acting out their unhappiness."[10]

Clearly, plenty of people simply aren't lit up by what they do every day. Many people feel trapped in a job that drains passion from them. At best, they feel intense ambivalence toward it. At worst, they hate it. They show up and go through the motions, droning on day after day, week after week, year after year, eventually forgetting the passion that once fueled them so long ago. And the thought of fulfilling what they're meant to do, if it ever existed at all, has long ago been shoved aside by the tyranny of the urgent.

Let me be candid: if you are in a job you aren't passionate about, you may need to start laying out a plan to pursue another path that better aligns with your passion. In my experience, if you can align your passion with what you do at least two-thirds of the time, there's no need to panic and jump ship. If not, you may need to make a move.

But before you do, I suggest you get clear on your passion first, because the problem may not be your job or organization at all. The issue may be that you don't have clarity about what lights you up or don't know how to align that passion with the greater purpose of your organization.

How do you temper the "grass is greener" mentality with the discovery of what you were meant to do? After all, it's one thing to be in a job you hate. It's another thing to be in a job where you do well and make good money, like I was doing with the construction company, but lack respect for the leader or passion for the work. That's a trap that keeps good people paralyzed every day. They choose to remain a cog in the wheel rather than find and focus on what lights them up.

InSPIRED leaders discover what they were made to do and then pursue it with abandon. So, my question is this: *if you're going to do anything in life, why not do something that lights you up?* The beauty of this mindset is that the brighter you are, the brighter you make your world. I want to do something that lights up the world. I want to light it up in a way that lights others up and encourages them to live out their unique brilliance. That's why I walked away from a good career to build a great life.

Let me be clear: I'm not advising everyone to quit their jobs tomorrow—or ever, for that matter. Not at all. In fact, what I am suggesting is that the disengagement so many people feel is a direct result of the disconnect between personal passion and organizational purpose. The responsibility to close that gap lies both with the individual to get clear on his or her passion *and* with company leadership to create a culture that resonates with a bigger and better *why.*

PASSION DRIVES ENGAGEMENT

It's difficult, if not impossible, to fully engage in anything long-term that doesn't excite you. And that can happen in any job. When we started this InSPIRED journey, I challenged you to tap into what inspires you, but inspiration and passion are a little different.

Inspiration gets you started but, unless you have passion, it won't be sustainable. Passion fuels you. It takes you from "I am motivated" to "I must!" You can be inspired by something stirring within, but still not be moved to do anything. Inspiration often happens from the outside in, but passion happens from the inside out. While inspiration is more esoteric, passion is more concrete. That's why you need to tap into the P in the InSPIRED model—passion. I am influenced and elevated by inspiration, but I am moved by passion to take compelling action.

In the larger organizational picture, a passionate workforce is an engaged workforce. When people understand the mission and buy into the larger purpose of the company, when that larger purpose aligns with personal passions and purpose—look out!

Consider an organization known for superior customer service: Chick-fil-A. This mighty restaurant chain started as a single diner called The Dwarf House. Led by its founder, Truett Cathy, it grew into a renowned brand that generated $9 billion in sales in the most recent year *with only 2,225 restaurants.* By comparison, the sandwich chain Subway earned $10.8 billion in sales, but it had over ten times the restaurants (25,908).

If you've ever been to a Chick-fil-A, you probably remember the experience as a pleasant one. Their customer service is intentionally over-the-top. For example, employees are trained to respond, "My Pleasure" when thanked. This seemingly small gesture signals their relentless focus on service and taps into the passion and *why* that runs throughout the entire organization. It was Truett Cathy's belief that "we aren't in the chicken business; we're in the people business." Cathy's leadership instilled the belief that his restaurants should be a source of encouragement to others. His personal passion and values became core organizational drivers.

Chick-fil-A leaders since Truett passed away have continued to share that passion and connect with his story. The walls of every restaurant share the Cathy story and the emphasis on putting people first. At Chick-fil-A, superior customer service focus stems from passion and purpose—and superior performance follows. InSPIRED leadership drives passion in the workplace, and that passion drives sales and fuels your sustained efforts.

PASSION FLOWS FROM PURPOSE

Where an organization has the *paycheck-prevailing* mentality instead of the *purpose-pulling* mentality, it doesn't have inspired engagement. It lacks the critical energy needed to power up and power through. Organizations find it difficult to integrate and execute well when leaders lack a cohesive *why*. The *why* drives a shared passion that fuels inspired, day-to-day activity. Entire organizations lose their passion when they forget their purpose.

But an organization is only as good as its individuals. So, do *you* have that internal flame, the fire that fuels and lights you up? In Truett Cathy's case, the *why* wasn't to be super successful or make a lot of money. It was to create a restaurant that valued and encouraged people—both customer and employee—and consistently delivered excellence.

It all starts with self-awareness and discovering what lights you up. What do you most enjoy? What's your personal mission or mantra? What are your values? These are active, concrete, and motivating. If you can unlock these concrete motivators in yourself, then you can unlock them in others and transfer passion. Your passion becomes such a driving, infectious part of who you are that you simply must share it with others in a positive way.

And passion has a ripple effect. Think about the impact you could have if everyone in your organization walked in the door every day brimming with a shared passion. If your organization employs 300 people, that's 300 families or 1,200 people on average who would benefit directly from a mom, dad, or significant other coming home every day fired up and ready to truly engage life.

One company I work with employs 85,000 people worldwide. Thus, when I coach the 15 executives on their leadership team, they, in turn, impact the 120 senior leaders. These 120 senior leaders impact the 1,000 regional leaders. These 1,000 regional leaders impact the 85,000 people that make up the rest of the company. And those 85,000 people all engage their families, friends, and communities every day. That's potentially millions of people impacted by something I say and do with those 15 executives.

> Entire organizations lose their passion when they forget their purpose.

That's the ripple effect of passion. It's why I got into this business in the first place, because I believe I can make a difference. What we all want are successful organizations where—after making a great contribution—moms and dads go home and treat family members better as a result of what they experienced in the workplace. We want a culture where people feel more motivated to live better outside of work because of the InSPIRED organizational culture they work in every day. That's the vision I have every time I walk in the door to a C-Suite office. And here's what I've learned: instilling passion, when coupled with InSPIRED operational excellence, will maximize shareholder value!

Ever wonder if your business culture is on the right track? Ask yourself these passion-related questions:

- Are your employees' children happy that their parents work for you?

- Does your organization contribute to the family fabric or tear at it? Do parents (your employees) come home stressed and embittered or powered up and ready to be fully present?

- Does your organization unintentionally send people home so stressed they don't have time to think about their passions?

Like it or not, regardless of your industry, if you're in leadership, you have to be passionate about people—and their passions—as a prerequisite for success.

HOW TO FIND YOUR *WHY*

Let's start by focusing on your individual passion, and how to identify it, before addressing the organizational *why*. After all, you may not be in a prime position to do much about your larger workplace culture, but the one person you can and must take responsibility for is you.

To begin with, many people don't embrace their passion, because they have no idea what it is. They live what Aristotle called an unexamined life. Consequently, they bounce around like a boat adrift in a stormy sea at night. They frantically row in one direction, following what they think is a lighthouse—only to discover the light was just moonlight reflecting off a wave that now threatens to capsize them. Without a clear purpose, nothing guides the way.

> Many people don't embrace their passion, because they have no idea what it is.

Because passion flows from purpose, you've got to be able to answer the question: at the end of my life, what do I want people to read on my tombstone? When you know what you want to say *with* your life, you can control what gets written *about* your life. For example, when generations of Fullers ask about me, I want them to hear that I was passionate about people. I helped businesses make a difference in the way they lead their employees, and in doing so, I positively impacted the lives of countless people I never met. In short, I want it said that I made other people better.

> When you know what you want to say with your life, you can control what gets written about your life.

To get clear on your purpose, you have to invest some time into thinking about what words you want etched on your tombstone. The words may not be chiseled until after you are gone, but you write those words with the actions of your life each and every day. That's why you have to gain clarity about your purpose while you still have time to change your direction.

3 STEPS TO PURPOSE

Your purpose is largely made up of three components: what you're passionate about, what you're good at, and the sweet spot where you can make a living bringing those two together.

- **Your Passions.** Start by listing all the things you would do for free simply because they make you feel fulfilled. Remember, inspiration may influence you, but passion moves you. When you're tapping into passion, think, *I cannot **not** do this.* What do you love doing so much that it doesn't even feel like work? But passion alone isn't enough. It has to align with the reality of...

- **Your Strengths.** Analyze your strengths and talents and factor them into the purpose equation. For example, you can be passionate about singing, but not be able to carry a tune in a bucket. You may long to be the life of every party but be wired to make your highest contribution in strategic thinking and reflection. In addition to taking assessments designed to uncover your natural behavioral style and wiring, consider these three things:

  ○ Know what you're good at—and what you're not good at.
  ○ Discover what energizes you—and what drains you.
  ○ Identify what recharges you—and what decharges you.

  For example, when I get in front of an audience and start teaching principles and helping people, something amazing happens. Even when I come into the room exhausted, I get reenergized by the experience and walk out with more energy than I had walking in. Not surprisingly, that strength zone is where you'll deliver your best results in…

- **Your Opportunity.** Where do your passions and strengths intersect? That's where you'll find a competitive advantage, a place where you can deliver something unique to the workplace and, for that matter, the broader marketplace. Your sweet spot is where you have the greatest opportunity to make your highest contribution, doing what you love in a way that is profitable to other people and rewarding to you.

Your sweet spot has to make sense in the marketplace, too, if you're going to make a living pursuing it. I've known many people who've launched into the speaker business by quitting everything else and simply declaring, "I'm going to be a speaker." It never lasts long.

People ask me all the time, *How do you do what you're doing?* My counsel is this: develop your sweet spot role on the side until your audience demands your full attention. That's when you can allow yourself to fully focus on your purpose-driven passion.

WHEN YOUR PASSION ISN'T YOUR WORK

But let's face it. Sometimes you may find yourself in a job or a role that just doesn't fit with your passions. You may be in the process of discovering your vocational purpose or you may just be in a season where you're doing all you can, but you don't have total clarity yet. When this is the case, and your work is not your passion, you have to tap into your passion outside of work.

Maybe you're passionate about music, art, your children, sports—you name it. Here's the perspective to bring an InSPIRED performance in those circumstances. Every passionate day you put in at work earns you a paycheck that enables you to engage your true passion. Let that passion outside of work be the fuel that drives you when you experience a disconnect at work.

Your organization needs you to bring as much enthusiasm and energy to your day as possible. Your full contribution there pays for the passion you really want to pursue. You either want to do what fires you up every day or do what you do at work well so that you can do what fires you up on your own time. Either way, the key to bringing full engagement every day is to tap into your passion. And who knows, maybe if someone sees you doing an amazing, inspired job, doors may open that allow you to do your passion full-time!

THE ORGANIZATIONAL *WHY*

Passion doesn't only drive individual engagement, it drives the culture of an organization.

When a company loses its purpose, people lose their shared sense of passion. How then does an organization find or rediscover its purpose? How does it get intentional about ensuring everyone shares that purpose and passion?

For starters, everyone in the organization needs to know why the organization was created. What was the founding story? What was the compelling argument for starting in the first place? What is the felt need that the company is serving now, and how does it connect with that single sense of purpose? Do you know the company purpose? Could you name the *why* behind the *how* and the *what?* And what about core values? Values are foundational to a leader's passion and an organization's purpose.

Here's a vital question for organizational leaders to ask: Are you still on track together, or at some point did everyone get distracted from the core mission, vision, values, and purpose?

Family businesses can be prime examples of what happens when the *why* gets lost over time. Grandparents carve a business out of the dirt with blood, sweat, and tears. At some point, the business gets handed off to the kids. When the second generation takes over the business, they know the passion Mom and Dad put into it, so they pour themselves into it. But, more often than not, the grandkids will

Is your organization mission-minded or messy-minded?

put that business in the ditch. Why? Because they didn't share the purpose and passion or see the price paid by that first generation. They don't share the passion, but they enjoy the privilege that has been their birthright. Unfortunately, birthright doesn't give passion and purpose. That's why so many organizations, not just family businesses, flounder and lose their way over time. They lose their *why*.

If you're a leader of an organization that has lost its way, you must discover where you got off track and how to get back to that place of purpose. Purpose and passion produce the energy required to build an InSPIRED culture. That's why TOMS Shoes has been so successful. Yes, they're selling shoes, but, more importantly, they have a social impact that drives them.

Purpose and passion are also why Michael Dell raised the money to buy his own company back. He was passionate about what he had created but knew he couldn't make the moves he needed to protect that purpose and passion if the company was publicly traded. So, he raised the money to buy back Dell stock and make it private again. That's what passion does.

> With a mission-critical mindset, people will elevate mission, purpose, and passion above the need for egocentric wins.

Passion tears down silos and positions organizational culture to be fully integrated, a topic we'll unpack more in the next chapter. When an organization isn't driven by passion that comes from a clear and honorable purpose, it's easy to get into a mess.

So the question is this: is your organization mission-minded or messy-minded? When you're driven by a good purpose and sense of mission, you don't have time to get involved in all the messiness— petty arguments, power trips, turf wars, and silo building. When you're all in you can't afford to take your marbles and go home when things don't go your way. When you know your mission and realize at a core level how important it is, you don't get caught up in all the distractions.

Do you have a mission-critical mindset in your organization or a silo-centric mindset? With a mission-critical mindset, people will elevate mission, purpose, and passion above the need for egocentric wins. It's not about who gets the credit; it's about getting things done to advance the mission. They don't look to place blame; they try to effect change. It's amazing how much can get done when no one cares who gets the credit.

When you have a strong sense of mission and focus on other people, you position yourself and your organization to function in a highly integrated fashion—fingers interwoven, arms interlocked, tearing down silos and moving forward together in pursuit of your shared mission. The question is simple: *what is your purpose?*

I believe the best teams need a dragon to slay or a princess to rescue. They can be galvanized against a common enemy (the dragon) or united toward a common goal (the princess to rescue). The former is more of a negative purpose in response to a threat, while the latter is a positive purpose in pursuit of an aspirational aim. Both can be effective in giving clear purpose and keeping teams out of the distracting messiness—but a word of warning about the dragon.

A team functioning in constant threat mode, motivated by fear of the next fire-breathing monster, can be damaged over the long-term. When people constantly feel threatened, an organization can actually regress as people begin experiencing a form of workplace PTSD that negatively affects performance.

Occasionally, organizations do face a real crisis that demands the slaying of a dragon. However, for long-term success, it's far better for an organization to cast a compelling purpose—freeing the princess—and then pursue it with a shared sense of passion. You must be realistic, of course, but always tie motivation to a positive purpose whenever possible in your leadership to bring out the most inspired performance.

LEADERS: SCREEN FOR PASSION

As a leader, to what extent do you have a responsibility to help people connect with the organizational *why?* I'll give you a hint: it's *all* your responsibility. You can't delegate passion back down to the employee. You must drive that purpose and continually refill the passion tank, because vision leaks.

You may not be able to completely control the factors that influence an employee's passion, but there is one thing you can do in the hiring process to ensure you get the best people who are most passionate about your cause—hire for values that match. Otherwise, you may generate passion for values that don't match your company.

As Jim Collins famously said, you want the right people in the right seats on the bus. But you must check their values and passion level before you let them on the bus in the first place. See if they align with your organizational purpose, mission, and values. If they don't fit, you simply cannot let them dilute the culture you work so hard to create.

Are you seeing why it matters so much to have clarity on your purpose and the organizational purpose? Purpose determines who you allow on the team. Purpose determines how team players play. Don't just accept any warm body. You want people who are raving, passionate fans. You want team members who remind you of William Wallace: "They may take our lives, but they'll never take our freedom!" You want people who share the same values and are passionate about what the organization does every day, you don't want people who are on the fence. You want them to be either in or out.

So, how do you do that? First, don't let people in unless they share your mission, vision, values, and purpose. It sounds simplistic, but it is vital. One of the biggest hiring mistakes leaders make is to bring talented people onto the team who are disengaged or lackadaisical.

Second, make the most of your onboarding process. What are you doing to infuse into them the story of how and why your organization was created? Can you tell the story so they become facilitators of the vision, mission, values, and purpose instead of just secondary passengers?

I encourage you to take the time to reconnect with the company purpose and review the current process to screen new hires. You'll save yourself a lot of trouble in the long run.

TOOL KIT

Summary

- Leaders must consider the place of values, purpose, and passion in their organizational culture and leadership styles.

- InSPIRED leaders discover what they were made to do and then pursue it with abandon.

- The disengagement so many people feel is a direct result of the disconnect between personal passion and organizational purpose.

- A passionate workforce is an engaged workforce.

- Think about the impact you could have if everyone in your organization walked in the door every day brimming with a shared purpose.

- Because passion flows from purpose, you've got to be able to answer the question: at the end of my life, what do I want it to say on my tombstone?

- Passion doesn't only drive individual engagement, it drives the culture of an organization.

- Always hire based on fit to the mission, vision, values, and purpose.

Startling Statistics

- 70% of employees in the US and Canada are not showing up to work fully committed to delivering their best performance.

- 52% of those workers are basically sleepwalking through their day.

- 18% of them are acting out their unhappiness.

Action Steps

- **Chisel your tombstone. No one lives forever.** So what do you want to be written on your tombstone? Think about what you prioritize now. Is that what you want to be remembered for? Write your tombstone in advance, and then live it out in such a way that strangers would be able to carve that message on your tombstone for you.

- **Define your passion.** Use the "sweet spot" exercise in this chapter to determine (or reconnect) with your passions. It's impossible to know if you are on the right track if you don't know where you are headed. Think about the things you value, and then brainstorm where your passions intersect with your strengths and the marketplace need.

- **Take the risk.** Life is too short to go through the motions. If you aren't living out of your passion, it's time to take some courageous steps forward. What can you begin doing that pushes you toward your passion? Take small steps and see where they lead.

CHAPTER 6

INTEGRATED

*"When everyone is on the same page, trust devel-
ops, and teams can grow and succeed together."*

—JERRY REINSDORF

They say competing in the America's Cup race is more like flying than sailing. Thanks to my passion for adventure, I can personally attest to that.

The America's Cup is one of the oldest trophies in yacht sailing competitions. The trophy was first offered as "the Hundred Guinea Cup" on August 20, 1851, by the Royal Yacht Squadron of Great Britain. Back then, the trophy was awarded for a race around the Isle of Wight. The winning vessel that year was *America,* a 100-foot (30-meter) schooner from which the competition got its name.[11]

These races are a marvel of collaboration and integration between man and machine, water and wind. Every sailor must work quickly and effectively to complete each job, or the entire mission is doomed to fail. Because one missed assignment can spell disaster, each person must be in peak mental and physical condition for the rigors of the race. The slightest hint of disintegration can result in an expensive defeat.

In 2013, the powerful yacht *Oracle* was positioned to make history in the America's Cup competition. In Greek mythology, oracles would give passing adventurers cryptic predictions of their fame or misfortune. It remained to be seen what destiny this six-man *Oracle* crew might create.

Flecked by saltwater spray, the crew of the *Oracle* flew across the San Francisco Bay. While sailors shouted directions back and forth from one carbon fiber hull of the catamaran to the other, skipper and helmsman Jimmy Spithill scanned the waters ahead with robotic precision. He knew every square inch of this two-ton feat of nautical engineering from the tip of its 13-story sail to the cutting-edge hydraulic foils.

Engineers and strategists had devoted years of innovative thinking and countless long nights to bring this ship to the pinnacle of racing technology. As soon as the hull hit the water, their job ended, and the crew's job began.

Defending the Cup would require experience, conditioning, and seamless communication. As four grinders—the brawny powerhouse sailors of the ship—turned two hydraulic hand cranks, the *Oracle* accelerated to breakneck speeds and began to levitate, rising out of the water on the thin hydrofoils that served as wings.

The thrill of that moment alone would have been worth the sweat and tears, but the crew had a higher goal. This race was for the match point. They had started the race in San Francisco Bay with the Golden Gate Bridge to the right and Alcatraz Island to the left. Each race included at least five legs across the San Francisco Bay. The teams would race until one crew outmaneuvered the other nine times. Once favored to win, these American defending champions now found themselves losing 8-1 to the challenging *Emirate New Zealand* team.

But as the catamaran hit the water's surface again, Skipper Jimmy realized the upwind third leg was approaching rapidly and with it his team's chance to overtake the New Zealanders. The *Emirate New Zealand* Kiwis were neck and neck with them and had momentum, morale, motivation, and numbers on their side. If the *Oracle's* crew lost this race, it would mean the loss of the America's Cup.

Jimmy had trained for critical moments like this all his life. Competing at this high a level—and even to qualify for the Cup—took years of sacrifice, study, sweat, and tears. But this native Australian, who taught himself to sail in an old dinghy his neighbors were throwing away, had always come back. He had been bitten by the seafaring bug passed down through generations of red-blooded adventurers who refused to settle for second place.

The America's Cup competition allowed for no margin for error—or credit for second place. According to yacht racing legend, Queen Victoria was watching the 1851 race of ships between the English coast and Isle of Wight. The surprising newcomer, *America,* suddenly pulled past the royal yacht to take the lead and dipped her sails to salute the Queen. I can only imagine the shocked Queen's reaction, because, according to legend, she leaned over to an assistant and asked, "But who is in second?" The assistant's terse reply captured the tense spirit of the competition ever since: "Your majesty, there is no second."

That same conviction powered Jimmy Spithill and the crew of the *Oracle* that day in the San Francisco Bay. Each man had his own strengths, his own job on board, and his own training regimen for the race. But they were united in one vessel with the single goal of victory for the entire team. If their integration were to break down, their entire mission would be in jeopardy. Understandably, Jimmy was feeling the pressure to do his part as they began the last leg of the race, zigzagging across the bay to make distance against the wind. With the defending champs' dreams on the line, Jimmy Spithill and his crew finally pulled ahead in the last leg.

And that's when it happened.

Kyle Langford had been a last minute addition to the team. The 24-year-old crewmember had only one main job on the *Oracle* on that leg—to hold a rope. It may not sound exciting or important, but this one rope kept the 13-story sail in place. When perfectly positioned, it could catch the wind precisely and propel the *Oracle* to victory.

As they sped confidently across the San Francisco Bay, the team was firing on all cylinders, just like they had rehearsed countless times. Then for some reason, maybe the salt water, sweat, or a momentary distraction, the rope controlling the sail slipped through Kyle's hands—and he grasped nothing but air.

Spithill watched helplessly as the rope slid from Kyle's fingers—knowing that one misstep now would doom all their efforts. Then the young Langford lunged instinctively for the rope and snatched the escaping line.

As the adrenaline rushed through him, Kyle tightened his grip further and looked back at his Skipper. Jimmy had seen it all. He raised a thumb amid the spray of waves as if to say, *Good job, mate!* The *Oracle* went on to beat the New Zealanders by 44 seconds, winning the race and securing the Cup for the Americans once again.

THE BEAUTY OF INTEGRATION

Langford's role may have seemed unimportant to the success of the team—until he almost failed to come through. Suddenly, his competency in rope-holding saved the day. His full integration with the rest of the crew made the difference between defeat and victory.

Integration, the fourth key to InSPIRED leadership, is a beautiful thing to behold. It happens when everything is working seamlessly with nothing out of place, when every qualified person does his or her job. Things just click and everyone takes pride in a job well done. Like the teeth on gears that line up perfectly and keep things running smoothly, integration is vital to the success of your team or organization, and to the inspiration of your workers.

Disintegration, on the other hand, is the downfall of many leaders, teams, and organizations. Like rusty gears with missing teeth, disintegration gums up the works and ensures you and your team remain frustrated and operating well below your potential. There's a reason we use the word "disintegrate" to describe an explosion. Disintegration leads to chaos and crisis. If left unchecked, it can undermine everything, including the best of intentions and the greatest passion. When the players and pieces don't seamlessly integrate, you get, at best, friction. At worst, total disaster.

What Jimmy Spithill wanted on the *Oracle* that day in San Francisco Bay was seamless integration, the confidence that every team member would do his part. He almost didn't get it—and the near miss would have squandered an otherwise heroic come-from-behind effort.

When teams are integrated and functioning properly, the results can be truly inspiring. Think about the no-look pass in basketball. Go ahead and Google "best no-look passes in basketball." I'll wait.

What did you see? A highly trained athlete dribbling the ball down the court, when, as if guided by some sixth sense, the player suddenly flips the ball behind the back or across the court into the ready hands of an open teammate who sinks the shot. Boom! Nothing but net.

But what appears to be a thing of beauty can be a disaster if the team isn't integrated. In that scenario, a no-look pass can result in a costly turnover or a bloody nose when the person isn't ready to receive the leather missile.

The mishaps can seem tiny when they happen, like a rope slipping through tired fingers or a pass deflected off an outreached hand, but they can have big implications. For as many times as I've had the privilege of helping teams and companies get integrated, I've also seen how easy it can be to overlook an important piece of the process—that slippery rope.

For example, I once worked with a team who had developed and installed a new computer system they just knew would improve customer interaction. They developed the entire program and rolled it out—only to realize they never involved a critical stakeholder group— the employees who would actually use the system to serve customers. Once the frontline employees began using the program, the lack of intentionality around design, testing, and use of data became painfully obvious. Because the employees hated the new system, it actually ended up damaging customer service and grinding down productivity.

Were the employees simply resistant? Not likely. They simply had not been integrated into the design, testing, and wisdom contribution. That problem was on the leaders.

> How many times have you thought, It really shouldn't be this hard to get things done? When you do, know that you have identified a point of disintegration.

Disintegration can plunge even the best organizations of all sizes into chaos. You may have had similar experiences of end users not being integrated into the design-build process, or key stakeholders not being brought in early enough. If you interact with other people in the workplace at all, you likely know the pain of wasting countless hours in redundant meetings only to find out the right hand didn't know what the left was doing throughout an entire project.

You may have gotten the runaround between departments trying to track down what should have been readily available information. I'll bet you've struggled to get two leaders on the same page when contradictory communications blew up over what should have been a simple project. The unintended results? Wasted time, project delays, budget overruns, and competing expectations. The list could go on and on.

How many times have you thought, *It really shouldn't be this hard to get things done?* When you do, know that you have identified a point of disintegration. Don't bury those thoughts. Heed the signal that your team isn't properly aligned somewhere. *It truly isn't supposed to be this way.* You're not crazy.

Thankfully, you can avoid million-dollar mistakes before you lose any more time, sleep, or your most precious resource—people.

GETTING FULLY INTEGRATED

A leader with a disintegrated team is like the emperor with no clothes. Everyone knows about the problem, except the leader. If team members believe stress, struggle, and production pain are just "how it's supposed to be," they'll continue to suffer and unintentionally underperform—until disaster strikes.

While disintegration is not sustainable, integration changes everything. I'm not talking about perfection, but rather the alignment, understanding, and adaptability of the group for the mission as it unfolds in real time in the real world.

So, what kinds of things need to be integrated? Here are a few examples:

- Culture and values into hiring, on-boarding, and daily activities
- Management modeling with daily habits

- Strategy and strategic approach with marketplace wants, needs, and reality

- Product and service offerings with customer wants or needs

- Strategy with organizational capabilities and capacity

- Strategy and operations with systems and processes at scale

- People and processes

- Change appetite with change metabolism

- And much, much more!

Complete integration requires attention once again at three levels:

1. **You.** The first person you need to integrate is yourself. If you are scattered regarding a vision for your team or dysfunctional when it comes to your own ability to get things done, you can't expect everyone else to have clarity. Leaders set the tone and pace for their team. So, ask yourself: *How am I integrating with coworkers, team members, customers, mentors, other influencers? And where do I need to step up my game?*

2. **Your team (internal customers).** Once you've addressed your own integration challenges, consider the integration of your own team with others in the organization. Integrated teams are drawn together holistically on a shared mission. So, ask yourself: *Do I know the critical people I need to integrate with? Do I intentionally reach out to peers? Do I know what their behavioral style is and how best to integrate with that style and communicate in their language? Can I trust them to have the know-how and flexibility to either get the job done or to communicate their problems? Do they trust me?*

3. **Your external customers.** How integrated are you with your external customers? Customer integration means you know your target audience well. You are on the same page with them and understand their problems, pain points, needs and wants. So, ask yourself: *How accurately am I working to solve real customer problems with my product or service before they even know there is a problem? How easy am I to do business with? How seamless would customers say our interactions are? Do customers come back to us? Do they tell others about us?*

When you intentionally integrate fully with yourself, your team, and your customers, everything starts to run more efficiently. Zombies disappear and work gets done.

PINCH POINTS AND THE 30% RULE

As a general rule, for every 30% of growth, an organization needs to reinvent its systems and processes. Integration is the key, but it has to be intentional and wise. It's easy to get bogged down in the details, to be so consumed with a cog that you neglect the rest of the clock. So take a moment to step back and zoom out.

Jocko Willink, retired Navy SEAL officer and author of the book *Extreme Ownership* says that in battle and in business it's critical that a leader be willing to step back to get a clear understanding of the situation, assess what he or she sees, and only then move forward to take decisive action.[12] As you can imagine, in the high stress of battle, stepping back may seem the opposite of what you should do. As an experienced, battle-tested leader, Willink knows it's impossible to fully integrate if you can't see the big picture.

As a leader, you must look at your workload and workflow in full. When you know the process from tip to tail, then you can create reality-based solutions. You can identify and stabilize your pinch points. These are the difficult places where problems continually rear up.

When you identify the *critical* pieces, you can make those the first priority for stabilization. If a patient were bleeding out, but also had a broken arm, no good doctor would mend the arm first. He or she would stabilize the patient—your team or business—and deal with the critical components first. These pinch points may vary, but here are some of the typical reason for breakdowns:

- Violated Trust
- Deficient Systems
- Miscommunication
- Conflict/Disagreement
- Lack of Competence
- Multiple Missions
- Lackadaisical Effort
- Fuzzy Vision
- Overwhelmed People or Processes
- Vague Expectations
- Lack of Training
- Micromanagement
- Unclear Expectations
- Growth

That last item—*growth*—may surprise you, but growth is one of the greatest causes of disintegration. All sorts of problems occur when organizations don't have a plan to adjust as they grow. Some people say *If it ain't broke don't fix it.* But if teams refuse to guide growth, they will end up broken with systems that no longer work.

Maintenance is the key to integration. If you don't maintain your Maserati, it will break down the same as any old lemon. As you grow, so must your processes. Every healthy and growing business needs significant reform. One company I worked with was struggling to integrate effectively in spite of doing well over $100 million in revenue. I asked a company partner, "When was the last time you revamped your processes?"

"About five years ago," he replied. I asked what revenue was five years ago. They were proud of their growth. He immediately answered: "About half that."

I blinked a few times before asking, "So, you're using a $50 million process for a $100 million dollar company? How's that working for you?"

It wasn't. They weren't broken yet, but they were experiencing significant disintegration because they had nearly doubled in growth without adjusting for it. We began to back up and figure out what methods *should* be in place to run a $100 million company and integrate greater numbers of employees, customers, resources, etc. Then we created a plan to implement these new processes and systems, while already planning what might be needed to support the *next* 30% of growth.

We see this 30% growth concept throughout life, but somehow leaders struggle to embrace it. Who still wears the same clothes they wore back in middle school? Styles change. Bodies change. Clothes get old and rip. When a business is growing like an adolescent, its systems must change to grow with it.

Many companies come to me with the fear that they are broken. I ask them, "If we dialed back business by 30% would you still be broken?"

They usually exclaim, "No!"

They're not broken in total, they are simply broken at scale.

> The team usually knows where the disintegration is taking place.

How much scaling have you blown past without changing or adapting your integrated systems, processes, and procedures? Are you using outdated modalities? That system overload can cause anxiety, relational difficulty, and customer dissatisfaction. Interestingly, the team usually knows where the disintegration is taking place. To start the conversation, ask your team these questions:

- If you could change anything about us, what would it be?

- If you could change three specific things right now about how we operate, what would that look like?

- What are your biggest pain points in how we do what we do right now?

Armed with the composite wisdom from your team, you can then ask yourself the same questions. Where are you personally feeling the disintegration? It won't be hard to tell because, like a pebble in your shoe or a front tire out of balance on your car, those will be the areas causing the most frustration and pain. Then look at how you've scaled with your growth. Have you grown as your sales have grown, or are you still doing things the same old way? What policies and procedures that used to help you are now hindering you?

Be certain you shift from "let me blame the person" to "let me evolve the system" or maybe "let me eliminate some bureaucracy." As you focus on integration, remember it's up to the InSPIRED leader to map the mission, look at the pinch points, and then make adjustments at every segmented step.

THE 4 KEY COMPONENTS OF TEAM INTEGRATION

Integration is the axis on which everything else turns. Get it right, and systems, processes, workflow, interaction, growth, and direction will fly with precision. Every team will need unique adjustments tailored to their purpose and environment, but some core elements will always be necessary for making progress in any situation.

Four key components of integration are needed on every team and organization that wants to execute with excellence:

1. Trust

Trust is the currency of leadership. It starts when your team can trust you *and* you can trust your team. It expands when other departments in the organization trust you as a leader *and* trust your team to execute on its promises and responsibilities. It expands even further when your external customers trust you as an organization to deliver a solution to their needs *and* to do so in a valuable and timely manner.

Integration without trust is like a boat without a keel. The keel is the strong backbone of a ship, made out of wood, metal, or other sturdy material. It juts down into the water beneath the boat like an upside-down shark fin and can weigh tons. In fact, a keel can make up almost half of the overall weight of a typical sailboat. It needs to be sufficiently heavy to stabilize, while being light enough for agility and adaptation at speed. You might think that something so heavy would immediately sink the ship. Instead, the weight works as a ballast, keeping everything balanced in rough waters.

Trust works in the same way. When you have a team you can trust, through good days and bad, you may wobble, but you won't keel over. Integration must be built on this core value of *trust*. On the other hand, mistrust creates isolation. Isolation in a team environment always leads to disaster. So, ask yourself: *Does my team trust me? Do I trust my team? Do external customers trust us? Do other departments within the organization trust us? Do I know what my team can and can't do—and how to grow where we are lacking?*

There are two types of trust—relational and transactional. When most people think of trust, they think of *relational* trust, because trust begins and ends on the strength of relationships. Every team has some sort of relationship history and these interconnected relationships either build up or erode trust. Trust isn't created in a vacuum. It's built over hundreds of little moments of interaction between real, complex people with emotions, feelings, and fears. Thus, a powerful component of relational trust is positive intent—choosing to believe the best of team members first, and then doing the necessary research into a problem.

When any team struggles to believe the best of one another, communication breaks down, and growth grinds to a halt. The absence of relational trust makes everything exponentially more difficult to do. But there's another sort of trust that is equally necessary.

Transactional trust means you believe that a person or team can execute on your expectations, follow through, and get things done. It differs from relational trust in that you may trust someone to be a good person with the best of intentions, but whether or not they can be trusted to get the job done is another matter entirely. You may have people on your team whose integrity and ethics are top-notch, but who, unfortunately, lack the skill and competence to complete the task. That's a breakdown in transactional trust that must be remedied.

In your business efforts, you're either going to have results or excuses. So, which does your team create most of the time? Do you trust each other to deliver results? When it comes to transactional trust, if someone promises to get something done, can you believe them? Can you calendarize it? If you can't trust people or teams to deliver the results they promise, you've both got a big problem.

In a business, transactional trust makes up a large part of the ballast that keeps the ship upright. If you have a person on your team that isn't getting it done transactionally, that's a place where you aren't integrated and something needs to change. The temptation can be to keep giving the benefit of the doubt and avoid the confrontation, but that doesn't do anybody any good. To build trust, you've got to address the problem and provide the training or guidance necessary to improve the situation.

2. Competence

Trust can only take you so far when you've got a competence problem. The sailing teams that race in the America's Cup can reach speeds of over 52 knots (around 60 mph!). Gliding over the water at that speed can feel like flying, yet they do it *without* motor or oars. It's all done by human power harnessing whatever the wind gives. To reach these speeds, four people work the hydraulic cranks at all times during the race—turning endlessly to control the hydraulic fluids that move the sails to correct the course.

Because victory rests quite literally in the hands of the crew, every member has to be competent to be effective—no exceptions. The sailors must trust the competence of their engineers and technicians to have built a swift and sturdy ship. The engineers must trust the competence of the sailors to control and power it. Everyone must trust the skipper to competently strategize and direct. The best and most beautiful yacht in the world is useless to someone who doesn't know how to sail. At that level, competence must be integrated with scale. Just because someone is competent to sail a 12-foot dinghy, it doesn't mean they're able to sail a 72-foot foiling catamaran. A Ferrari in the hands of an inexperienced teenage driver is likely to end up crashed on the side of the road, while an experienced racer would make the same car hum around every corner.

As an InSPIRED leader, you have a responsibility to create and guide a *competent* team. That means you've got to understand your team's core competencies. So, what are your core functions and core competencies? These questions can help you figure that out:

- What is it that your department *does?*

- What are the *critical deliverables?*

- What are the *critical roles?*

- Within the critical roles, what does competency look like?

You then have to assess the skills of each member of the team and position them for maximum value and production. Identify their areas of strength and weakness and put them in the best possible position based on their skill set and ability. As you analyze your workload and workflow for competency, here is my four-part process:

- Know what needs to be done

- Break it down into various job functions

- Identify the critical deliverables of each function and consider the key KSAs (Knowledge, Skills, & Abilities) needed

- Hire or train people to deliver those KSAs

By the way, competency starts with you. Ask yourself: *Am I competent in getting my team to that next level? If not, then no one can trust me to stay the course and deliver results.* Iditarod teams who race their sleds through snow and ice in Alaska can only move as fast as their slowest dog. Your team is only as strong as the weakest link. You'll want to commit to ongoing development to make sure that weakest link isn't you.

3. Commitment

We have to have the competence to do what we do effectively. We have to have the commitment to do it with full power. I once saw a guy wearing a T-shirt that announced, "Talented but lazy." What kind

> Until everyone commits, you're not really a team.

of a brag is that? Talent is a gift. What you do with that talent is your commitment—to yourself, your team, your organization, and to your customers. If your team doesn't have your commitment to go all-out, you're just creating drag.

If the crew of the America's Cup competition wore those T-shirts, they wouldn't be the crew for very long. Commitment is not only the key to their being a team, but also the key to victory. The training lasts for up to four years of daily grind. Their commitment to the one goal is what differentiates them as a racing team and not merely a group of people sailing on a nice yacht. Until everyone commits, you're not really a team.

We all start with some level of competence, but knowledge in any industry has to be learned. Give me a person who has some level of competence, but is trustworthy with a heart full of commitment—and I can turn that person into a vital and integrated member of the team. You will gain competence every day if your heart is committed.

> You will gain competence every day if your heart is committed.

Relying on the commitment, work ethic, and honesty of your employees and partners frees you to embrace the areas of business that are your greatest strengths—no cumbersome micromanaging required. But don't get me wrong—it's crucial to know everyone's limits. If you're always overloading the team with commitments, expecting them to be overcommitted to your aims at the expense of other critical life priorities, you're draining trust right out of the bucket. Be careful to protect their passion to commit.

4. Communication

People have been figuring out ways to communicate with each other since they first set foot on the earth—from cave drawings and hieroglyphics to modern day emojis. We've become masters of getting our ideas across. Without dialogue, our teams disintegrate. But communication requires more than the transmission of information.

On a boat flying across the bay, crew members must become efficient and effective at relaying information. Wasting time and energy, or worse, risking miscommunication, just won't do. In your business, what are your critical communication points? Do you speak to employees or team members in person or via video calls? Will a team member text you with a question, call you, email you, or wait until you come asking? How does your behavior influence how willing teammates are to communicate with you? Every interaction is a potential miscommunication unless you are intentional about integrating.

Integrated communication depends on doing it in ways others understand and appreciate. Does one member love to contact you directly? Give them a chance to do so. Are they independent and work on their own until checked upon? Be sure to check in on them at regular intervals. It's impossible—and not necessary— to get everyone to speak the same language. Do your best to integrate with the people you lead and speak to them using their preferred style.

It's also important to identify the key people with whom you need to communicate the most—and help leaders on your team do the same with their key personnel. Everyone needs a leader who will hear him or her. As a leader, you must take responsibility for communication as far as it is within your control.

When I'm working with turnarounds or start-ups, I like doing critical communication in morning huddles. These are short team meetings designed to communicate critical information, focus the team, and get back at it. To make sure you are communicating effectively, consider these questions:

- What are the critical components I need to communicate?

- What does my team need to know?

- Whom should I tell first?

- Are there any critical communication points being missed?

- Is my communication one-way or two-way?

- Is the message I'm trying to deliver the message that's being received?

All communication is not created equal. Many leaders technically say all the right information—but they're still not communicating. They're just *transmitting*. They've mistaken leadership monologues for company dialogue. Then, when they encounter problems, they blame the team—but the problem may be self-inflicted. Communication means not only that transmission has occurred,

> Communication means not only that transmission has occurred, but also that recipients have received the information—and they know what to do with it.

but also that recipients have *received* the information—and they know what to do with it.

In the military, when somebody has given an order, the soldiers respond back with a term called "Hooah!" It stands for H.U.A. Heard. Understood. Acknowledged. Effective communication asks for an echo check from the team, a confirmation that not only have they heard, but they understand what to do, acknowledge their role, and are moving to action.

LEADERS: INTEGRATION BEGINS WITH YOU

You may not be a leader in the military. Your team may not fly like Jimmy Spithill's crew of sailors. However, you are responsible for equipping your team to run at an integrated, day-to-day level. At its core, communication begins with you. Are you talking *with* your team or *at* your team? Is communication one way or actual? Integration runs on dialogue.

All teams will have problems. But the solutions depend on where the problem originated. Integrational snags fall into one of two categories: relational or systemic. Keep both in mind to get the full picture. With breakdowns in *relational integration,* the problems are between people. Relational disintegration isolates. It creates false assumptions and expectations. It stirs up frustration, anger, shame, and withdrawal. It makes the mission impossible to achieve. Relational disintegration involves each of the four major integration components above: trust, competence, communication, and commitment.

Are mistakes being shouldered by managers instead of discussed with employees? Teams with relational integration value talking about mistakes and problems instead of shaming. They create solutions together. Relationally-integrated teams trust each other to come through on commitments, voice opinions, share struggles, celebrate strengths, and be honest about needs and production.

Breakdowns in *systemic integration* result in problems with team structure, processes, and logistics. These problems tend to repeat. If something happens once, it's weird. If it happens twice, it's suspicious. If it happens three times, it's very possibly in need of a systemic solution. Systems are meant to support not strangle. So, where your process frequently experiences pinch points, back up and look for an integrated solution.

But remember to watch out for unintended consequences that result from your solution. Don't serve a half-baked idea. Be sure you understand the downstream implications and integrate with your team and other stakeholders first, so you can solve the systemic problem, not create a new one.

The most important thing to realize is that integrated teamwork begins and ends with leadership. Model integration for your team. Make it a priority. And you'll enjoy plenty of first-place—even come-from-behind—finishes of your own.

TOOL KIT

Summary

- When teams are integrated and functioning properly, the results can be truly inspiring.

- Leaders set the tone and pace for their team.

- Every healthy business that sees substantial growth needs significant reform.

- As you focus on your integration, remember it's up to the InSPIRED leader to map the mission, evaluate the pinch points, and make fresh adjustments at every segmented step.

- Trust is the currency of leadership.

- Integration must be built on the core value of TRUST.

- There are many ways to communicate, but they come back to one basic thing: being willing to speak in a language others understand.

Startling Statistics

- As a general rule, for every 30% of growth, an organization needs to reinvent its systems and processes.

Action Steps

- **Integrate through trust.** The best teams have one thing in common: trust. They know that they can rely on each other to do the job well and get the job done. If you don't have that trust built into your team, find the problem and fix it. Trust is built over time with integrity and honesty. Start by being trustworthy yourself. Next, look for ways to give other people a chance to be trustworthy with you.

- **Hone your communication.** If you are talking and nobody is listening, you aren't communicating. Perform a communication audit. Ask your team members to rate your communication skills, and take what they say to heart. Then perform a listening audit. Work to listen to your team member and implement their best input—be sure they know you are hearing them.

- **Evaluate how your team works.** Teams need relational and systemic integration to function well. As a leader, evaluate your team through those two lenses. If your team isn't relating, what can you do to foster trust? If the systems aren't optimized, where do you need to change them?

- **Learn the Behavioral Style of each member on your team.** By doing so, you can understand how the collective behavioral styles impact integration. Visit RightPath.com to get started.

CHAPTER 7

REAL

"Whether an effective leader acknowledges problems within an organization, or an individual recognizes areas in need of personal growth, resilient people use failure as an opportunity to spot their weaknesses."

—Amy Morin

M y team and I once came alongside a group that had acquired a manufacturing plant from a well-known conglomerate. When the new leadership entered the picture, their initial review of the financials and operations revealed a startling truth: they believed they had a million dollars of inefficiency creating a significant drag on production and profitability.

So, they did what a lot of leaders do. They started cutting the budget to trim costs. Unfortunately, one of their first moves had been to cut the workforce and reduce retirement benefits for those who remained—not the quickest way to build relationships. Leadership then went to those same employees, with the best of intentions, and asked them to find that $1 million in inefficiencies to further cut costs.

By then, labor was in no mood to be helpful. When we entered this scenario, it was clear there was a lot of relationship healing and trust building to be done between the workforce and management. They had gotten intentional about cutting costs, but had done so at the expense of their most valuable resource: people.

After doing a deep-dive diagnosis, we developed a program to help restore trust, rebuild relationships, and get everyone on the same page. We worked through leadership issues at every level, from one-to-one to group training sessions, to address the people issues.

Eight months after we wrapped the initial pieces of the program, leadership discovered something startling when examining their quarterly numbers: management and labor together had found and eliminated $800,000 of inefficiency! Once the relationship challenges had been addressed and trust rebuilt, it got easier to focus on getting results. It wasn't that no one knew where to find the inefficiencies. They simply were not inspired to do so. Leaders had caused the workforce to disengage. Their actions disincentivized their ability to eliminate extra costs.

After working with us, their leadership was empowered to lead the organization in an InSPIRED fashion—and got the results they believed they could achieve. But first, they had to get Real. They had to get relational.

InSPIRED LEADERS ARE REAL PEOPLE

How do people experience you and your actions? It's an intriguing question because it causes you to pause and reconsider everything you think you know about yourself and your interaction with others. It means you have to think not only about what you intend by your words and actions, but how your words will be received, perceived, and experienced.

Everything—from how you carry yourself when you step into a room, how you listen when someone is talking, make eye contact, react to feedback, say your favorite leadership mantras, encourage or discourage—creates an experience that either inspires or exasperates.

> Lead where you're strong, team where you're weak

Unfortunately, most people lack self-awareness. They prefer to remain blissfully ignorant and blame everyone else for any problems they create. They fail to realize how their words, actions, attitudes, and approach impact performance and relationships with the people they interact with on a daily basis. These leaders may know their strengths, but they overuse them to their own detriment. That's not good enough if you lead people, if you aspire to be an InSPIRED leader.

Another adventurer, Captain William Bligh, exemplified this lack of awareness. He possessed a strong ship, a schooner crewed by forty-three talented Royal Navy seamen. He had charted a clear course and mission. He may have even succeeded in accomplishing the mission if he had been an InSPIRED leader who understood how to manage relationships with his crew.

But Bligh had a reputation for looking out for himself. Historical accounts tell us his crewmen described him as a stern, overbearing, and critical leader—frequently successful in achieving objectives, but harsh with punishment. He was focused, but either not self-aware or, more likely, he just didn't care.

Sailing on an 18th Century cutter ship was no vacation. In 1787, Bligh and his crew, along with Bligh's comrade and leading lieutenant, Fletcher Christian, set sail from England on a ten-month journey. They were bound for Tahiti and its famous breadfruit harvests. They reached the island, but instead of purchasing, loading, and leaving with his precious cargo right away, Bligh allowed his men to stick around for five months without any direction or discipline. Bligh refused to understand and manage his people in ways that led to success for the whole team.

Bligh never took his eyes off his prize—making it to the West Indies to resell the breadfruit and make a pile of cash. His devotion to the mission, however, blinded him to wise execution. Rather than respect his people, he crippled them. He left his sailors so idle for so long that they adjusted to relaxed island life.

When he piled his men back on board *The Bounty* after months of rest and socialization with the Tahitian women, he expected instant results without instituting any processes.

The problems began immediately. His men grumbled and complained to Lieutenant Christian about leader Bligh's strict discipline and exhausting expectations. British historian Richard Hough notes Bligh "failed to anticipate how his company would react to the severity and austerity of life at sea … after five dissolute, hedonistic months at Tahiti."

Bligh had a people problem. He certainly engendered no trust from his crew. But at the core, Bligh failed to manage expectations in relationships and lead his people well to readjust to a disciplined life at sea. He had permitted his men to get cozy doing nothing and now had a group of men who resisted his hard-nosed efforts to get them working again.

Bligh responded to the crew's resistance with an even harsher crackdown. Only three weeks into their journey home, *The Bounty's* frustrated crew, including Bligh's comrade Fletcher Christian,

slipped into their captain's cabin, tied him up at cutlass-point—
and set him adrift in the Southern Pacific.

Bligh's story has become legendary through various retellings of
the infamous "Mutiny on the Bounty." While you probably haven't
set your boss adrift on the open sea, or been marooned by your
employees, you've likely been tempted to do so.

When a leader fails to lead people well, his team and mission
will fall apart. Even talented teammates, like Bligh's crew, will rebel.
Through another series of adventures, Bligh eventually made his way
back home. Unfortunately, he didn't learn his lesson. His unwise and
demanding leadership style led to three more mutinies.

INSPIRED LEADERS ACHIEVE RESULTS WITH TEAMS

Maybe you think, or even know, that there is a certain way you
are *expected* to act, so you put on a persona each day you walk into
the office. You want to be the real you, but you're so busy figuring
out the *right* thing to say that you forget the *best* thing to do—be real
and authentic to who you are. Inauthenticity drains your energy and
renders you ineffective.

Even more importantly, if you're not comfortable with and can't
get along with *you*, how in the world are you going to get along with
anybody else? It's a key life principle, not just a business one. That's
why I encourage leaders to have their people use self-assessment
tools, like RightPath Resources®, so everyone gains an awareness who
he or she is and how best to work together.

Everyone is wired for greatness, but everyone is not wired for
greatness in the same areas. For example, if you are a blunt, get-it-
done person, you may be great in crisis management, but not so great

where the situation calls for empathy and patience such as mobilizing the day-to-day habits that create a profitable workplace. That doesn't mean you're inferior or defective. You're not weak, but you're weak *in that role.*

Weakness is more a role-fit than anything else. We do need to learn to stretch, grow, and adapt. But if we are spending most of our time and energy out of our strength zones, we'll run into trouble and wear out everyone around us. Genius and flaws exist in each of us, and neither one has to diminish the other. If you know where your genius lies, but struggle in one particular role, you can create a multifaceted team. Lead where you're strong, team where you're weak. Don't have someone to team with? Lead where you're strong and put a system where you're weak!

It's time to admit you can't do it all. And you're not expected to! No one expects you to know it all, do it all, or be it all. But the people you lead do expect you realize that truth.

I help leaders all the time who say, *I can't admit weakness to my team or tell them what I'm not good at.* In a sense, the joke is on them, because their team members already know their weaknesses. Think about it. How hard would it be for you to rattle off the top five things your leader *doesn't* do well? Pretty easy, right? So why would you assume that your direct reports can't do the same? You aren't hiding your weaknesses from them when you won't admit them. They know your weaknesses better than you do. That's why you need to be authentic. You're not fooling anyone.

It takes humility to admit, "I am not amazing at this, so I should partner with someone who is." Humility multiplies strength. Pride isolates people and breaks down teams. The humble leader, rather than trying to do it all, functions like an air traffic controller who scans the radar and calls certain team members to move depending on the strengths needed in any particular situation. If inauthenticity has created a rift between you and your team, you're missing out on their support to cover your weaknesses and maximize your strengths. Remember: leaders are to achieve results with—and through—their teams.

THE EQ FORMULA

Daniel Goleman is the father of the term *emotional intelligence.* *Harvard Business Review* released an in-depth study that interviewed thousands of top leaders across a wide range of industries to determine how much of their success was based on technical acumen (IQ) and how much was based on people skills (EQ or EI). Based on the results of the study, a doctoral student created a formula to represent the findings:

IQ + EQ = XQ (ability to execute)

This team discovered that your IQ plus your EQ equals your XQ, or your ability to execute. Your technical acumen plus your people skills determine how effective you're going to be as a leader. It's not always the smartest person in the room who leads best.

When I do in-person workshops, we do an exercise during which everyone fills out sticky notes about the best leader they've ever worked for. They write what they remember most about him or her and then stick the notes all over the room. We then sort the answers to reveal the same startling answer every time: as little as 10% of the positive that workers recall is about what their leaders *knew.* The other 90% has to do with the leader's emotional, social, and relational actions. In other words, good leaders engage people authentically to interact with them and bring out the best in their teams.

Daniel Goleman's study found that a leader was typically most successful with a mix of only 15% technical acumen (IQ) and 85% people skills (EQ). Don't miss this: the people you lead think your people skills are *five to six times* as important as your technical skills or knowledge. That's the value of getting Real. It's not that IQ is not important. It's the table stakes that get you into the leadership game. EQ is what keeps you in the game and elevates your chances for success.

> Good leaders engage people authentically to interact with them and bring out the best in their teams.

So, are you willing to get real and relational in order to be effective? Your people and your company need you to. You have to first be honest with yourself and discover where you need to improve.

THE 4 QUADRANTS OF EMOTIONAL INTELLIGENCE

If you want to understand how people experience your leadership, you have to begin with one fundamental truth: people will interpret you emotionally *before* they interpret you logically. While you may want them to look at you with logic and objectivity, it won't happen. Not at first anyway. In short, they'll evaluate your emotional intelligence and how much you seem to care before they ever care about how much you know.

It may help to think of the following four quadrants of emotional intelligence:

1. Self-Awareness
2. Self-Management
3. Social-Awareness
4. Social-Management

EQ: Emotional Intelligence

The four together form an interdependent relational chain. If you want to be an InSPIRED leader who empowers a team to perform at its highest level of execution—one who is authentically real—you've got to learn to master all four quadrants.

Self-Awareness

It's a funny thing to realize how unaware we really are about ourselves. You may think, *Of course I know about myself. After all, I am myself.* But truthfully, it's more comfortable to gloss over the ugly bits and focus on what you've always assumed to be great about you.

Because you use these assumptions to think about yourself, you may be wearing a set of emotional blinders. You can live and work for years with those presuppositions—until you get intentional about awareness. You have to turn your head to see the full landscape.

Get intentional to focus on what's really going on with you. You may need a mirror. Have you ever had a parent, spouse, or friend look at an outfit you selected and ask, *Is that really what you're wearing?* The look on their face says it all—what you thought about your looks was all wrong.

At some point, you need the same relational check, a look in the leadership mirror to understand how other people experience you.

As a leader, your intentions matter, but not nearly as much as your teammate's perception of the interaction.

You may think you're simply being blunt or honest or both, but it all gets perceived through the prism of interpretation. It takes self-awareness to know what message you're really sending to your team and what your message does to company operations.

Our bodies have protections in place for when things become a little too intense. In moments of intense emotional overload—like when you're being "honest" with one of your direct reports, or when your manager is being "blunt" with you—a part of your brain can get hijacked by this defense mechanism. The messages fire up your spinal cord right into the amygdala. Your logical functions shut down and instinct takes over. Sound familiar? It's the fight or flight response. At every moment, your biological sensors are trying to determine whether to fight, flee, or weather the storm.

Now here's some additional physiological awareness for you. The emotional or limbic part of your brain moves 80-100% *faster* than your thoughts. Consequently, in stressful situations, you'll feel first—and want to react—before you've reasoned out your best course of action. It's a defense mechanism that has kept our species alive for millennia, but it certainly throws a wrench into change management and workplace interactions. It takes an intentional, mature person to be actively self-aware and understand, *I have been triggered and want to react, when what I need to do is choose to listen.*

These keys to good self-knowledge feed great self-awareness:

- **Take a RightPath Behavioral Style assessment to understand your own hardwiring.** Do people take energy from you or give energy to you? What's your default communication style? Will you work better with the big ideas or are you a details person? Knowing how you are wired helps you better interact with others. (Visit InspiredLeadership.com/Assessments)

- **Understand your energy gainers and drainers.** Based on your natural hardwiring, identify those things that are likely to put you into a state of confusion, frustration, or distraction. Using a journal is a great way to identify patterns over time. It will also help you remember things that affect you but may not be remembered long-term. Look for trends, patterns, and emotional triggers that affect your success. Those are key pieces.

- **Monitor your physiological responses.** Stress manifests in your body. Stay mindful of how you feel and physically respond. Your palms may get sweaty, or you might feel warm or flushed. You may feel your heart racing. Your back may tense. If you feel the symptoms of an adrenaline rush, you're probably in an emotional state of hijack. If you're aware, you can prepare and not be held captive anymore. After you identify these things, dig deeper to ask, *Why does this take me here? Why did this situation trigger that reaction in me? What emotional state was I in and why?* By understanding the contributing factors, you can intentionally choose your response—and with it, the consequences you cause.

- **Get some third-party feedback.** A trusted observer or advisor is better than gold. Don't find somebody too similar to you, because you may share the same blind spots. Find an objective third party who doesn't lose or gain anything by giving you advice. They can serve as a sounding board for your decisions and responses. Additionally, 360° assessments are a great tool to capture that feedback and yield tremendous insight into how others experience you.

- **Personal reflection.** No one knows you like you know you, even if you don't realize how much you know about you. Personal reflection helps you pause and listen to what's going on in your mind so you can make sense of it all. It means being honest with yourself that you are a work in progress and to focus on what you can do to be more honorable.

Self-Management

Becoming *aware* of who you are is the first step, but you then must learn to *manage* who you are. Unfortunately, most of us get hijacked by the emotion in the moment and don't seek to understand what's really happening. What can you do to circumvent your own biology and enhance your self-awareness? It helps to realize you are always holding two cups in your hand. One contains water, the other gasoline. When situations arise sending people into your office with their hair on fire—which one will you throw? It's your choice.

One of the best ways to manage yourself and avoid escalating situations is to build margin into your day. Do you tend to fill every last moment of every day with something to do? Most leaders I encounter have no downtime. Yet the only way to avoid emotional overload is to intentionally build margin into your day.

One simple way to do this is to keep a five- to ten-minute buffer between meetings. If you go from meeting to meeting, back-to-back, you'll bring emotions and triggers from one meeting to another—all day long. Your lack of margin will hijack your results as you find it increasingly difficult to respond well throughout the day. On a good day, you'll keep it bottled in until you get home—then take it out on whomever you encounter there. Not good.

Another key to self-management is identifying existing stress triggers. When you can plan beforehand what is on your plate, and even identify people in your day who give you particular frustration, you can prepare healthy exit plans and backup decisions.

Finally, learn to manage expectations. Expectations without communication lead to frustration. Think ahead about upcoming events (you need margin to do this, too!) to achieve the right level of expectations. Then put a plan in place to adapt, rather than react, in that situation. You can see problems coming beforehand if you take the time to prepare well.

The question isn't *are* you going to get triggered, but what's the recovery plan for getting to a better state when it happens? Identify whatever it is that stimulated you. Then figure out if you can slow the situation down and take a five-minute break to regroup. Any time you create space to recover, you slow the momentum of your runaway emotions.

If you know that you're going into a potentially difficult situation, have a pause strategy as well as an exit strategy on hand. For example, if you know you're about to have a difficult conversation, consider setting the meeting fifteen minutes from when you have a hard stop. This gives you margin to give yourself a natural exit strategy. (For more thoughts on self-management or coping mechanism, visit InfluenceLeadership.com.)

Social Awareness

Once you focus on understanding and managing yourself, you can't stop there. You need to develop your social awareness and management, as well. It's time to turn your attention to others to learn, recognize, appreciate, and understand *their* emotional state of being. Lest you still think emotional awareness of others doesn't matter, remember this: people are hired for what they know. They're fired for how poorly they relate to others.

> People are hired for what they know. They're fired for how poorly they relate to others.

One talented IT supervisor I knew managed to get hired *and* fired within sixty days. He came into a maturing startup as a tech wizard with serious credibility. Everyone knew he knew his stuff. So as soon as he arrived, he started pointing out everything the coders on his team were doing wrong. He didn't pull any punches, just brash tone and told them they need to toughen up and do better. Within a month—a month!—all twelve coders collectively turned in their resignations to the CEO with a simple directive: either he goes or we go. Guess who went? He had the IQ, but not the EQ. He failed to exercise social awareness and read the situation better to take a wiser approach.

Having all the right answers won't save you if you miss this crucial point. Leaders without social awareness won't last long—and won't keep their top people around long either. Talent always has a choice. They can do what they do anywhere. So why would they do it for you? If you refuse to develop your EQ, your poor people skills will drive away your "A" players and be left with mediocre talent who puts up with you because they don't have anywhere else to go. The harsh truth is: Every leader gets the team they deserve— *eventually!*

The Gestalt Theory essentially says "human perception is not just about seeing what is actually present in the world around us. Much of what we perceive is heavily influenced by our motivations and expectations."[13] Everyone has the potential to interpret situations differently. When it comes to interpersonal awareness, this understanding of human behavior is critical. It allows you to understand those interpretations and react accordingly. The way you act or communicate may be crystal clear to you, but the way that communication is received and acted upon will depend on the filter through which they view you. What's each person's lens through which he or she sees you or the situation? As a leader, you need to get to know those lenses, acknowledge new perspectives, and respond accordingly.

> Talent always has a choice.

One key to increasing your social awareness is to understand that communication doesn't function on a straight line back and forth between people, like a string between two tin cans. In fact, linguists have identified several components of communication, called speech acts, that create—and easily confuse—our communication. They are:

- **Locution**—the audible words you *actually* say or physical gestures you make.

- **Illocution**—the message you *meant* to convey with those words or actions.

- **Perlocution**—the *recipient's* interpretation and actions they take because of it.

Imagine you're at a dinner party sipping delicious soup, but it just needs one last thing. You look up from your bowl and ask, "Excuse me, is there any salt?" Your words, taken quite literally, have to do with whether or not salt actually exists (locution). But any savvy partygoer would pick up on the message you meant to convey by your words (illocution) *"Is there any salt on this table, and, if so, can you pass it to me?"* The resulting action (perlocution) is, hopefully, a successful passing of the salt to flavor your soup. However, if you kept asking, "Hey, is there any salt?" and your friends simply replied,

"Yes," and kept slurping their gazpacho, you'd get annoyed with their lack of awareness.

Speech acts explain how two identical sentences can have very different meanings based on context and intent. For example, "Oh no, *I'm* not mad at all!" and "Oh *noo,* I'm not mad at *all!*" lead to two very different conclusions. The first might leave you wondering who else you might have made angry, while the second sarcastic reply might move you to retaliate. These challenges explain why most of our communication isn't actually achieved through words themselves but instead through tone, context, and body language—and why social awareness requires you to go deeper to find out what your team—consciously or unconsciously—is really communicating.

> Every leader gets the team they deserve— eventually!

The number-one way to pick up on that is by listening the right way. Which do you tend to do?

- **Passive listening.** You're in the room but distracted and not fully engaged. As a result, you tend to not recall critical information.

- **Pretending to listen.** You act as if you're paying attention, but lack the will to empathize. Instead, you give an occasional nod or "uh-huh." This type of listening (or non-listening) can be recognized and felt as non-caring.

- **Selective listening.** You pick and choose information to retain based on your personal bias, discounts, dismisses, or disregards. As a result, you often misinterpret others, but don't find out until it's too late.

- **Active listening.** You are intentionally attentive, empathetic, and seek to understand the *why* behind someone's words. You'll often play back your understanding of what you heard to ensure communication has taken place. This form of listening requires more energy but demonstrates that you value the person and their words.

In addition to actively listening, you also need to "zoom out" and read the room. Start by knowing and understanding each person's natural hard-wiring (behavioral style) then observe body language and positioning. If you can be the first one in the room, read everyone coming into the room and make a note of what's going on with them. Then note how they react or respond in the meeting. What does their body language tell you? Are they harried and flustered? Light and engaging? Stoic and silent? Are they responding to real or perceived threats?

Then look for false agreement (or giving in). Does someone stand up for his or her opinions and communicate directly? Does another someone get trampled easily, pretend to agree in the moment, or get quieted as the conversation continues?

Finally, look for physiological clues. Does someone show physical signs of emotional overload or stress? Are they flushed, sweating, breathing quickly, looking around, blinking rapidly. They might be speaking calmly, but tune yourself to their inner state by reading their outer disposition.

If possible, or if you have time and the situation makes sense, seek a trusted advisor. I've often been asked to sit in on important meetings with leaders simply to observe and read the room. You want somebody who can objectively interpret the social signs so you compare perspectives.

Then choose your response. Do what's right. This is where trust and respect really matter. If you have the emotional intelligence to see when someone is stressed or troubled, you have a responsibility, too. Some people abuse that information to get what they want. But an InSPIRED leader knows that doing what's best for their teammate or partner might also be what's best for the team as a whole.

Adjust wisely to respond responsibly. You can offer someone a lifeline by offering different options or attempting to dial back a confrontational situation. When someone feels that a leader understands their perspective and is willing to help find a winning solution, they not only trust that leader more, but are also more willing to get real to help the team win.

Social Management

Now you've read all the pieces. Social management has been likened to a bank account. We are constantly making deposits and withdrawals. It is crucial you make sure the account stays positive at all times!

> Social management has been likened to a bank account. It is crucial you make sure the account stays positive at all times!

You have yourself. You have the business and team. You have everyone else. How do you put all this together for more successful outcomes? All integration and inspiration comes down to managing those social interaction points between individuals; your team's function is up to you. You are responsible to weave your people and work into the beautiful but complicated web of business culture. To navigate it, you need not only authentic social *awareness* skills, but authentic social *management* skills. Here are five key tips:

1. Know the dynamics and impact of behavioral styles.
2. Take emotions out of the driver's seat.
3. Show respect to everyone.
4. Gain their perspective before sharing yours.
5. Practice active and empathetic listening every time.

You can be as right as the day is long, and be the smartest one in the room, but if you can't help your team work together, you've got a full tank of gas in a car with no wheels. It's one thing to be right; it's entirely different to be effective. Likewise, you can point out every little misstep (like the IT manager did) and assign guilt. But that won't solve problems. Don't wallow in the mud pit. Find and fill it.

It's easy to believe that your emotions, your perspectives, and your history are real and irrefutable. But maybe not. Before you go into a big meeting or difficult conversation, realize which topics are based on fact and which are based on opinion. No one is going to agree on everything. But sometimes you just need a general direction that aligns with the mission. Then you can compromise, reevaluate, and find solutions a little farther down the road.

Emotional intelligence means properly managing people and situations. As much as possible, remove the emotion and get back to helpful actions. When you guide people back to the facts, you guide people back to what's fixable. When you recognize the frustration, you can identify what you can't control and move back to what you can. If you can learn and use that skill, it will help you as a leader and tremendously help your organization. Good social management enables you to guide everyone in the room towards responsiveness instead of reactivity.

> It's one thing to be right; it's entirely different to be effective.

Sometimes you can avoid the problem entirely the next time by taking preventive steps. Did you know that after experiencing rudeness or social problems at work, it takes a person twenty minutes to refocus again?[14] That's both damaged relationships *and* productivity lost. Think about that the next time you are tempted to say something snarky to one of your team members. If you want to manage social awareness, nip this behavior in the bud by putting a code of conduct in place or even offering problem-solving training to employees.

Frustration is a function of expectation. So what have your team members come to expect from their interactions with you and with each other? When I go to Atlanta to see clients, if I expect to be able to drive on Atlanta freeways and average 50 to 60 miles an hour, I'm going to be severely frustrated. Why? Because there are 600,000 other cars going in the same direction. My expectations are not in alignment with reality. Your expectations about your interaction with your team have to align with what's reasonable and possible. Figure out what you can change right now and what you can't. I can't control the 600,000 people that are driving where I'm driving, but I can control my emotions or my expectations in that particular scenario.

> High-functioning, high-performance teams function on a high relational level.

Social management can only happen when you stay fluid. Bruce Lee said, "Be water, my friend. Be Water." When running water comes across a stone in its path, does it stop? Bunch up on one side? No, most of the time, water adjusts around it—or carries the rock along with it.

InSPIRED leaders have a code that guides them and allows them to operate with integrity. There are certain non-negotiables when it comes to your authenticity and character. Being emotionally intelligent is one of these. High-functioning, high-performance teams function on a high relational level. They can navigate the tricky waters of communication. They don't judge each other; instead, they assume positive intent. They verify intent if needed, trust each other's integrity, *and* collaborate fully because they are REAL with each other.

You don't always have to be right; you don't always have to be the last voice heard in the room. So stop putting effort into that. Instead, decide to navigate the tricky waters, remove blinders, and see yourself as others see you. Listen well, react wisely, manage the room, and most importantly, bring out the best in your team and in your leadership.

TOOL KIT

Summary

- Everything you do—from the way you carry yourself when you step into a room, to the way you listen (or don't) when someone is talking, to how you make eye contact, react to feedback, say your mantras, encourage or discourage—creates an experience that either inspires or exasperates.

- Everyone is wired for greatness, but everyone is not wired for greatness in the same areas.

- Genius and flaws exist in the same person, and neither one has to diminish the other.

- People will interpret you emotionally before they interpret you logically.

- One of the best ways to manage yourself and avoid situations that escalate is to build in margin.

- It's one thing to be right; it's entirely different to be effective.

- Learning natural, hard-wiring, behavioral styles is critical to leadership success

- The lens through which we and others interpret every situation can and does "bend" each person's perception of reality.

Startling Statistics

- Daniel Goleman's study found that a leader was typically most successful with a mix of only 15% technical acumen (IQ) and 85% people skills (EQ). Your people skills are *five to six times* as important as your technical skills or knowledge.

- The emotional or limbic part of your brain moves 80-100% faster than your thoughts.

Action Steps

- **Examine the experience of *you*.** Commit to understanding yourself this week by thinking about how others experience you. Consider your body language, facial expressions, word choice, tone of voice, unspoken expectations, and their reaction. How would you feel after an encounter with you?

- **Admit your weakness.** You may be tempted to not own up to your weaknesses. But everyone on your team already knows what they are anyway. Take an honest look at where you aren't being real. Then look around at your team and see who has a strength in an area in which you are weak. Empower them to use their strength to the entire team's advantage.

- **Adjust and respond.** Learning to be real is all about making little adjustments over time. Once you understand the experience of you and admit your weaknesses, you can make the micro adjustments that make you a better leader. Look for ways each day to be authentic and lead in an InSPIRED way.

- **Visit InspiredLeadership.com/Assessments and receive a discount code to take a RightPath Profile Assessment.** Understand your hard wiring and how it impacts everything you do. I believe so much in this assessment that I am reducing the price of your assessment by $25. (Essentially, I am refunding the cost of this book if you will take this critical learning step.)

- **Deploy a RightPath LQ360 Assessment.** Understand how others are experiencing your leadership now and enjoy the same $25 reduction in the price of an LQ360 assessment. Visit InspiredLeadership.com/Assessments for your discount code.

CHAPTER 8

EXECUTION

"If you are going to achieve excellence in big things, you develop the habit in little matters."

—Colin Powell

ditarod. The name has become synonymous with tenacious execution in the most grueling of circumstances.

The race for which the Iditarod is named first ran in 1925. It began as a life-and-death mission to get life-saving serum from Anchorage to Nome, Alaska. Innovative thinking as well as courageous leadership forged the path and made history across dangerous terrain. Dog teams led by hardy mushers had to navigate quickly but effectively through snowy passes and icy mountains—all in the unforgiving Alaskan winter.

Today sledders and their dog teams must use similar innovative thinking, iron-will perseverance, and courageous leadership to execute the Iditarod race. The competition still kicks off in Anchorage. Each team of dogs must be fed hundreds of thousands of calories a day, a feat that requires strategic supply stops. Training and tactics vary with some teams running in the day and others at night.

To complete the race—in one piece—requires strategy and execution, leadership and teamwork. One thousand plus miles of harrowing terrain later, teams cross the finish line in Nome. Just like in the workplace, grit, determination, and agility are required to win. But remarkable results only become possible when they execute all of it at just the right time and in just the right way.

In 2008, I embarked on my own Iditarod adventure. I traveled nearly 4,700 miles over six days, stopping to speak to corporate leaders along the way about the challenges and rewards of inspiring leadership. I eventually flew from Seattle to Anchorage, up to the frozen region of Kotzebue, and then to my final destination: Nome, Alaska. I wanted to mush a team of dogs—just like the Iditarod racers do—to experience a little of what those hardy souls go through to lead a team to get it done.

As a greenhorn (newbie) to dog mushing and sled racing, I had to find a patient but talented teacher who would show me the ropes. Nils Hahn, an Iditarod veteran, agreed to be that mentor. He even helped me intentionally prepare for the trip. For example, I initially thought I had the right equipment because I had a pair of hiking boots from a popular, name-brand manufacturer. Nils simply laughed and told me I would need to bring something much, much warmer if my feet were going to survive the adventure. He was right. The massive moon boots he recommended successfully kept my feet warm.

In many ways, Nils challenged my understanding of what leadership is—in the context of his world. For example, my experience caused me to reconsider a statement I had repeated for years: "If you're not the lead dog, the view never changes." Sledding with Nils quickly taught me that the true leader of the dog team isn't out in front. The lead dog may be the leading *in* the team but the leader *of* the team is back in the sled. He or she is back in the sled executing on vision and strategy.

Another thing *was* certain for that real leader: the smell doesn't change either. One of the minor details no one thought to share with me was that when the dogs take off, they get excited. So excited, in fact, that they immediately relieve themselves. It's a routine part of the racing experience and one that encourages mushers to stay *on* the sled.

After running the first team for several trips, I started to feel like I was getting the hang of things. Nils asked if I was up for adding dogs to speed things up. The feeling of speed as you fly across the snow is exhilarating. So, true to my adventurous-but-without-thorough-evaluation nature, I agreed: "Let's go for it!"

I admit to being a little nervous. My team consisted of valuable, veteran Iditarod dogs that belonged to someone else. I felt the weight of their safety as I stepped onto the sled, breathed the crisp Alaskan air, and consumed the beautiful scenery. I was exactly where I wanted to be, blurring the line between reality and fantasy on this adventure!

It seemed like Nils moved in slow motion as he leaned down, pulled his snow hook from the ground, and started his team of sixteen dogs out of the kennel. That was my cue to release my own hook and follow. My mind was racing as I realized this was going to be a more powerful and dangerous experience than I had anticipated. If I executed well, this would be the ride of my life. If not, at least I would land on snow.

The body of a dogsled includes the basket where cargo or people can ride. The musher stands right behind the basket, either on the drag, a flat, mat-like surface, or on two protruding sticks called *skis*. By standing on the drag, the musher can slow the team with gentle resistance; he or she achieves maximum accelaration by standing on the skis.

To stop, the musher steps down on a metal U-brake that pushes several 9-inch spikes down into the snow. With the research I had done,

I knew that each dog could pull about 300 pounds. I had seven dogs, which equated to 2,100 pounds of pull. I weighed only 185 pounds, so as we headed out, I couldn't help but feel a little uncertain about whether I could control this team.

The adventurous voice in my head said, "Let's go!" But my body said, "Heck, no!" As a result, instead of starting with two feet on the drag, which I had done to perfectly execute several sled launches before, I planted one foot firmly on the U-brake.

Within a moment, we hit a turn. We clipped the top of a tree buried in the snow with only the top three inches exposed. As my weight shifted, the U-brake spike bit into the snow and caught on the buried tree. I flipped off and over, desperately trying to live out the #1 rule of mushing—*never let go of the sled!*

As the dogs dragged me through the snow, my first thought wasn't the brightest one: *How did this happen, Fuller? Just flip your body and the sled will flip with you.* My second thought brought me back to the reality of my failed execution: Twenty-three dogs just started out on the trail ahead of you—*dodge the land mines, Fuller!*

Ten seconds into the mission, and I was being dragged through a pile of dog—well, you know. Of course, it wasn't the dogs' fault that we'd gotten off to such an ugly, smelly start. Those dogs were just doing what they had been trained to do. If I, their leader, had been better prepared to execute at the higher level, I wouldn't be flailing in the brown snow desperately trying to regain control. The skilled dogs wanted to race, but they were dragging 185 pounds of dead weight. As a leader, my failure to execute hurt the team.

I wasn't prepared for the team's strength and feared failure. My rigidity took us down. Thankfully, Nils saw my predicament and slowed the dogs enough so I could right the ship, scamper back onto the mat, and regain control. The rest of our twenty-mile trip went smoothly. I needed a change of clothes at the end of it, but I was none the worse for the ride.

However, the experience reminded me of the many times I've encountered leaders in the workplace facing similar situations with their teams. They know where they want to go, but don't have the confidence or training to execute well. They have a mission and a team, but they end up face-first in a crappy mess—always scrambling to get back on their feet before other leaders see that they've fallen short.

If you're truly interested in InSPIRED Leadership, you probably have big ideas and dreams. You may feel inspired and eager to get out on the trail. That's good, because now is the time to put the pieces together. Because without proper execution, none of what you've learned to this point really matters.

EXECUTION GONE WILD

Most workers have experienced the pain that comes from a leader who simply can't get things done. Some leaders are so relational that they give little thought to production. Other leaders are simply unprepared to lead and end up in way over their heads. Still others don't know what they don't know. But a leader who doesn't execute isn't really a leader at all. Unfortunately, failure to execute affects more than just productivity and the bottom line. It causes relational damage, too.

> A leader who doesn't execute isn't really a leader at all.

Have you ever worked in a setting where the boss seemed to know where to go, but couldn't tell anyone else how to get there? Relationships break down with poor communication. The team can resent being held responsible for results they don't understand or aren't equipped to achieve.

On the other hand, maybe you've experienced an environment in which a manager hit the brakes too hard, too fast—as I did with my Iditarod team. Every turn seems to throw the team off course. Every bump becomes a crisis. Team members can't embrace their strengths or run with efficiency, because they're choked back by a leader who doesn't know how to execute. Even the best people have to work overtime to make up for a poorly executed plan.

Like I learned in Alaska, give conflicting directions to a team of high performers and they'll either grind to a halt or throw you off into the brown snow. Either way, the results will stink.

Lack of direction, definition, and subsequent re-work exhausts the team, leads to missed deadlines, and lowers productivity. About $1 million is wasted every twenty seconds due to poorly executed business strategies.[15] You might as well light your revenue on fire, because poor execution will send whatever you earn up in smoke.

> When trust leaves, commitment isn't far behind.

When you hamper productivity, blow through finances, and destroy relationships—even unintentionally, you create the unholy trinity of execution gone wild. In the end, when you fail to execute, you're not only hurting the bottom line, but also betraying the trust of your people. Who puts faith in someone who can't be trusted to complete the plan? When trust leaves, commitment isn't far behind.

If you promise an inspirational culture but don't deliver execution, inspiration turns to exasperation, especially for the top talent you need to stay engaged on your team. Remember, talent always has a choice. The best people want to get things done, not stagger in and out like zombies.

EXECUTING THE EXECUTABLES
WITH EXCELLENCE

At the end of the day, leaders and their teams are paid to deliver results. As a leader, you need to make sure your team members get the support they need to complete the projects with excellence. There is no substitution for execution. It's the catalyst for every element of InSPIRED leadership. Nothing will last without it.

To get intentional about execution, you have to do something counterintuitive: slow down. I tell leaders all the time to stay out of the weeds as a general rule; however, to execute successfully you'll have to get down into the weeds at least once in a while to understand the underlying processes and micro-behaviors that make up your organization's well-oiled machine.

> You're either executing with excellence or choosing extinction.

Think about how hummingbirds fly. These amazing wings move so rapidly they appear to be a blur of color. It's breathtaking—and looks impossible. They dart and zip around in ways that seem effortless. But slow the flight down one/one-thousandth normal speed, and you can see what the wings actually do to allow the bird to hover so perfectly. Likewise, when it comes to execution, it's only when you slow things down that you can see how every piece and part works together.

"Productivity is never an accident," says Paul J. Meyer. "It is always the result of a commitment to excellence, intelligent planning, and focused effort." When you first focus on quality in the micromovements, then quantity can follow. It may not be easy, but at the end of the day, you're either executing with excellence or choosing extinction. There is no third option.

When I was being dragged by the dogs in Alaska, I learned valuable lessons about how leading a team is vastly different than leading yourself. In a team of dogs, as with a team of people, everyone has a purpose and place. Again, Jim Collins calls this putting people in the right seat on the bus. When the dogs are in the right place, they glide across the frozen trail with grace and purpose and speed. But with Iditarod, you can only move as fast as your slowest dog. Similarly, you've got to not only position your team for success, but also *inspire* the team to work rapidly together to reach the destination.

What I love about the Iditarod dogsled race is that the race is nearly 1,100 miles. How do you inspire a team of dogs to run 1,100 miles, the equivalent of the distance from Chicago to Miami? How do you begin to tackle that big of a goal? Easy. You use checkpoints along the way. Pass through each of these checkpoints, one at a time, and you'll ultimately reach the finish line.

You don't worry about the distance. You understand it and plan for it. You train the team to run from one checkpoint to the next. Trying to focus on the full 1,100 miles would be debilitating. You can't afford to get emotionally hijacked about running 1,100 miles through the barren Alaskan winter. You need to simply focus on the 25 checkpoints that run from Anchorage to Nome and tackle them one by one.

> The key to executional excellence is compartmentalization.

The key to executional excellence is compartmentalization. During the race, each checkpoint provides a tangible and achievable goal to achieve as well as a place to refuel, regroup, and gear up for the next leg of the journey. If you don't plan ahead, you won't survive. The excellent way takes a little more thought, but it pays off exponentially in both the short and long runs.

Likewise, with your own team, you have to understand the big picture of where your team is going and then break it down into manageable components. These bite-sized pieces are the measurable markers that enable you to ensure the team is making timely progress. Execution begins at the molecular level when you can identify, componentize, and deliver all the elements that lead to the desired outcome.

The level of executional excellence baked into your company culture determines whether your model will fulfill or falter—whether your people lock up under overwhelming expectations or have the tools they need to reach big goals. The way to make sure your processes are executed smoothly is to componentize everything into the smallest actionable details. Then schedule it.

Consider this sales example. If your plan is to sell 10 items in a week, and for every 10 people you talk to one will buy, then it follows that you must talk to at least 100 people to reach your goal. Making 100 sales calls in a week may sound daunting. For some, it may even feel paralyzing. But what if you break it down into components? You have 5 workdays, so divide 100 by 5. That means you need to call 20 people per day. Divide that by two. Now you need to talk to 10 people in the morning and 10 in the afternoon. That averages to about 3 people every hour. That feels a lot more doable, doesn't it? Simply reach out to someone every 20 minutes and you'll stay on track.

You may not be responsible for sales. You may be responsible for production. The same rules of componentization apply. Define excellence. Break it down into the smallest possible steps that lead to results. Define what excellence looks like in each of these steps. Execute on those steps one by one. That's how all successful leaders operate. They keep one eye on the big picture and the other on the underlying fundamentals. Finding that balance keeps you moving forward and executing with excellence.

Execution really comes down to the rhythm of the run and understanding what people are doing on a regular basis. Financial reports are lagging indicators. Activity reports and daily habits are leading indicators or predictors. You can correct daily habits easier and faster using those. By adjusting daily to-dos, you can build new muscle memory and the smooth cadence of the right activity.

THE R.A.C.E. METHOD

To execute with excellence, you need to work within a framework. After my time mushing dogs in Alaska, I developed The R.A.C.E Method to capture the essence of how to get things done with excellence consistently. When I raced the dogs, I saw how this model worked and began to help people apply it to their business and leadership. The R.A.C.E. Method empowers you to execute with excellence.

Ready.

Are you and your team ready to produce at the highest level? If not, you may need to invite some consulting expertise to the conversation (yes, this is what we do). At the beginning in Alaska, I was eager to run, but I didn't know *how.* That meant I needed to find someone who did. In my case, it was the veteran Nils. I suspect your situation probably requires some different expertise.

In North American culture, we tend to value action over planning. Many businesses unofficially adopt the motto, "Fire, ready, aim!" The problem with this mindset is that it eliminates the planning and pre-planning needed to assure we reach our destination. I felt ready to race in Alaska, but clearly I hadn't thought far enough ahead.

> To be Ready means you plan ahead before you head out.

To be *Ready* means you plan ahead before you head out. You make sure you have a good team in place. You make sure they're well supplied for your run. You make sure you know where you're going and have a plan to make consistent, sustainable progress. In the Iditarod, being ready also means placing food, supplies, and other material at each of the selected checkpoints along the grueling 1,100-mile trip.

Action.

How well are you living out the InSPIRED components and unleashing your passion-fueled contribution each day? How well are you executing with excellence by integrating fully through effective processes? How well are you using Real relational skills so that your internal and external customers feel well served? In its simplest forms action answers these for your team:

- Do we know what to do?

- Are we equipped and empowered?

- Are we engaged and inspired?

- Are we doing what we know?

- Are we measuring what matters?

- Are we deploying positive accountability in a timely manner?

Action begins when you show the team where to go and how to get there. You start with your own behavior, because your actions determine what the rest of the team will do. If you don't guide them, you'll have an execution problem.

> Action begins when you show the team where to go and how to get there.

To take action, make sure everyone on the team knows their roles, responsibilities, and activities. When everybody's on the same page, doing the right things on a consistent basis, the action flows smoothly. When the leader understands the timing, then the team understands the execution, and they can be coached to the highest level of performance.

Action isn't an all-out sprint, but a measured process. There may be times you have a deadline to reach or a special project to tackle, but action is mostly a system of continuous activity and positive accountability. If you are always sprinting and functioning in panic mode, you'll wear out, burn out your team, and fall short of your goal. That's why you need….

Checkpoints.

When you're ready, it's easy to take action. It's also fun to see progress. But if you never stop to assess that progress, you can't be sure you're on course. Both in the Iditarod and in leadership, checkpoints are critical. They help you assess where you are, determine if it's where you should be, and provide opportunities to make micro-adjustments before you get too far off track. Checkpoints also allow you to pause and refuel, so you're ready for the next stage of the race. There will be both major or minor checkpoints as you componentize each stage and every task to be done within it.

Checkpoints may involve additional training, rest, or redefining the objective. The purpose of checkpoints is to:

- Ensure consistent progress in the right direction
- Refuel both physically and mentally
- Make adjustments faster or sooner
- Strategize

- Celebrate and coach

- Correct any operational behaviors sooner rather than later

Checkpoints also help you assess what did and did not work. If you want to execute well, you've got to measure your progress along the way. If you don't measure and report, then your results will be on accident, not on purpose. You may get where you intend to go, but you'll have no way to replicate that success. On the next run, you'll have to figure it out all over again.

As a leader at these checkpoints, your primary job is not to be a correctional officer, bringing down the hammer on all the team did wrong.

> Today's excellent is tomorrow's average.

Your job is to be a coach who checks in on performance and helps to elevate it in each person on your team. You still need to hold people accountable, but your role is to unleash the power of the team, not to wait for somebody to step out of line so you can snap them back into place.

Evolve.

Finally, to execute with excellence, you've got to learn to evolve. I wasn't the same person after I raced those dogs for twenty miles. I learned some things about the dogs and myself. In the evolving stage, you take what you've learned through the *Ready, Action,* and *Checkpoint* stages and apply it to the process. It's a matter of continuous improvement where you make field adjustments to people and processes so you stay on track.

One of the biggest issues I see when I coach leaders and organizations is an unwillingness to perform a healthy self-evaluation and learn from where they've been before. Like watching game films in the NFL, self-evaluating your performance is non-negotiable as part of a continuous improvement process. It's not done *to* anyone it's done *for* everyone.

Today's excellent is tomorrow's average. The sad thing is that there are as many positive lessons in the game films as there as negative ones. But if you never go back to evaluate your processes and systems, you'll never improve. If you are unwilling to improve, you can't become an InSPIRED leader who executes with excellence. Refusing to evolve is like having a four-inch binder full of wisdom left on the shelf covered in dust.

Don't let past mistakes (or past successes) define you. The next leg of the race will be totally different from the one that came before. That's why it's critical that you evolve and continue to bring out your best and the best in your team.

3 KEYS TO CONSISTENT EXECUTION

Let's take a moment to begin to unpack The R.A.C.E. Method by going into the weeds a little bit on the first step—Ready. In this Ready phase, I've found three keys to consistent execution excellence—goals, roles, and habits. These are the *what,* the *who,* and the *how* of getting things done. To get ready, you need to know what you want to achieve, who needs to fulfill which roles, and how you will function in the day-to-day to succeed.

Goals

Setting INSPIRED goals begins with asking these questions:

- Where do you want to end up?

- What is the order of the steps?

- Who does those steps best?

- How much time do you need?

- What are the best in your industry doing?

On the Iditarod trail, mush teams rely on trail markers to let them know how far they've traveled and how much longer they have to go. Even with these markers, some mushers have stopped fifteen minutes from the next checkpoint, because they didn't realize how close they were to achieving the next goal. In the middle of the action, it's difficult to tell one snowbank from another.

The same is true for you and your team as you execute. With your head down in the weeds, you can lose sight of where you are. That's why you need goals that serve as checkpoints. The checkpoints do two things. They help people focus on componentized goals and provide built-in celebration points along the way. Similar to the way the various camps on an Everest ascent provide visual cues to progress, your checkpoints let people measure progress toward achieving results.

I'm a big fan of looking at the delivery deadline (the goal) and working backward to create progress goals. If I want to run a twenty-eight-minute 5K race, then I need to average an eight-minute mile. If I'm not on that eight-minute mark after the first mile, I need to adjust. If you want to do a product launch in September, you'll need to retro-engineer the schedule to achieve that aim and set checkpoint goals. Likewise, when faced with a breakdown in a process, work backward to discover where the breakdown occurred and then set checkpoints to fix it and monitor progress in the future.

As you evaluate your goals in the harsh light of reality, you must consider your team's ability to deliver on those goals in that time frame, which leads to evaluating the roles needed and who will fill those roles.

Roles

When you're clear on your goals and you've set checkpoints to monitor progress, then you can start positioning your team for maximum success by examining roles. I suggest you begin with these questions:

- Who is actually doing and delivering?

- Is everyone crystal clear about roles and responsibilities?

- How does each person contribute to each step?

- What strengths does each person contribute and where will he or she do the best work?

In light of the role, what weaknesses does each person have and how can these weaknesses be overcome? (This is a great time to revisit the RightPath assessments I mentioned previously to make sure the right people are in the right seat on the bus.)

Do you need to add or remove people from the team? Have you first trained them to ensure removal is wise?

Sports teams are only allowed a certain number of players. You too must work within certain constraints such as budget and organizational restrictions. That's why it's so important to have the right team members in place to get the job done. An offensive lineman may technically be physically able to line up under center, receive the ball, and throw it to a receiver, but that's not what he's built for. In baseball, pitchers are notoriously bad hitters. That's not why they're on the team. The constraints actually help the team by forcing them to put the best players in the roles where they perform the best. Likewise, constraints help you ensure you put the right people in the right places to win.

That doesn't mean no one will ever have to do a job they don't enjoy or step out of their comfort zone, but it does mean that you position each person to be and deliver his or her best. A pitcher sometimes has to bunt a run in. Football players sometimes line up differently for a trick play. But your team is filled with people who will excel in their areas of expertise—and propel you to excellence—if you ensure they are in the right role.

Habits

Habits have the power to make or break your execution. As James Clear says in *Atomic Habits,* "You do not rise to the level of your goals, you fall to the level of your systems." Nowhere is this reality more apparent than in execution. You can have the noblest goals but, without systems in place to achieve those goals, you'll never get off the starting line. You'll do what you've always done and wonder why you're getting the same results.

To achieve excellence through execution, you've got to manage your own habits and then help your team members manage theirs. It goes back to the DITLO I described earlier—what happens in the *Day In The Life Of* your team. What habits, actions, and mindset need to be in place to achieve your optimal day? When you define your DITLO, you set your success parameters. Actions then become

> "You do not rise to the level of your goals, you fall to the level of your systems." —James Clear

simple. You know that if you do certain things each day, you'll move closer to your target. Do them often enough and they become habits. And good habits allow you to take little shortcuts to remarkable results.

So, how do you make the right things habitual for your team? Identify the right things to do, then make them repeatable, sustainable, and scalable. Start by answering these questions:

- **What's the workload?**

  - Does it come to you segmented or does it need to be compartmentalized?
  - Are there trends, patterns, and timing to follow?

- **What are the standard operating procedures (SOPs) that lead to successful execution?**

  ○ Do they exist by design or by default?

  ○ How effective are they? Are they current?

  ○ Do you know the steps in the process?

  ○ Do you know your strengths and struggles, efficiencies and inefficiencies?

- **What are your output expectations?**

  ○ Are there checkpoints to ensure you get the outcome you need and provide accountability?

Working through these steps takes time. It's not flashy, and it's not always fun. And that's why so few do it—and they fail to deliver excellence. But when you have answers to these questions, you can begin to work them into your DITLO and move to other steps in the process. Again, if you or your team need a proven guide to help you plan well in this Ready phase, just reach out. (Inspired@RightPath.com)

> The bottom line is this: you need to inspire to execute effectively.

The bottom line is this: you need to inspire to execute effectively. You must avoid exasperation at all costs. You can be intentional, passionate, real, have a heart to serve, and integrate well, but if you fail to execute you've failed to do your job. There's no substitution for executing with excellence. But if you work the steps with excellence, execution takes care of itself.

LEADERS: EXECUTION FOR YOU

It may be easy for you as an individual to think, "Execution really isn't my problem. It's an organizational problem." But here's the truth: if you are drawing a check from the organization, you have a responsibility to execute with excellence. In fact, I believe you have a mandate to return value to the organization.

If you want to be an InSPIRED leader, you have to take ownership. You start by asking *what can I do?* You have to determine where you are and how you can lead from the middle of the pack to influence others. In other words, decide to be an inspiring performer who steps up, not a prima donna who checks out when the going gets tough.

Make it your standard to be among the top 5% of performers at your job. Sadly, I've worked with teams where individual contributors have tried to slow down the entire organization to their speed. That's not what InSPIRED leaders do. Set your own high standards of excellence and then strive to live up to them.

If you don't have a personal standard of excellence, you've actually neglected the *P* of the InSPIRED Pathway—your passion and purpose. When passion and purpose are missing, there's nothing to fuel execution. By default, you'll execute with mediocrity, because you have no passion to do your job. It may be that you used to be passionate about your role, but you burned out. If so, you may need to unplug and reconnect with your passion and purpose. Nobody wakes up saying, "Today, I want to be average!" Be inspiring by executing with excellence all day every day to fulfill your purpose and live out your passion.

> If you want to be an InSPIRED leader, you have to take ownership. You start by asking what can I do?

Here's a pro tip: the key to executing well as an individual leader is to benchmark the best. Know what the best in your industry or area of expertise do, then adopt some of their best practices. Hold yourself to their high standards. Break down their best practices, then create habits to replicate what works in your own situation. Remember: *Find awesome and copy it.*

For example, when I was struggling as a young sales manager, I didn't know what to do. I asked my general manager for the phone number of the best sales manager in the company. I wanted to know how he led his team. I wanted to learn from the best, not try to stumble through it on my own. I knew I could jumpstart the process if I learned from the best. And so can you.

Execution for your team or organization starts with you as a leader. You have to execute well and bring your best as an internal measure of your integrity. You also have to make sure your people are executing well. You need to operate at 30,000 feet—but bring a pair of binoculars! You are responsible for resourcing the team, which means you actually have to be sufficiently in the weeds at some point to architect the best system possible.

Then onboard, resource, train, develop, hold accountable and do all the things that bring out the best in your team. It's a never-ending cycle of coaching, correction, reward, and discipline. RACE: Ready. Action. Checkpoint. Evolve.

An InSPIRED leader has to show the way by living out these leadership principles. Don't blame others. Take ownership—and lead. Remarkable results will follow.

TOOL KIT

Summary

- You've got to not only position your team for success, but to inspire them to work together to get to the destination.

- Componentization is the key to inspiring your team to peak performance.

- Take it one step at a time. Do the next right thing and you'll be pleasantly surprised at the results.

- If you promise an inspirational culture but don't deliver execution, inspiration turns to exasperation, especially for the top talent. They will leave.

- Your team is filled with people who will excel in their areas of expertise—and propel you to excellence—if you make sure they are in the right role.

- To execute well as an individual, you have to know what the best in your area do.

Action Steps

- **Define your finish line.** You can only execute when you know what you are executing toward. Define your finish line so you can get clear on the next steps to get there. Make it far enough in the distance that it challenges you, but not so far out that it is unattainable.

- **Identify your checkpoints.** Break down the steps you need to take to get to your finish line. There is no right number of steps; what matters is that each checkpoint is understood, effective, communicated to your team, and gives you the opportunity to recharge before pushing on.

- **Run your R.A.C.E.** Every leaders' R.A.C.E. looks different. Get ready by preparing your team to reach the finish line. With no excuses, take action by executing with excellence each day. Determine which checkpoints make the most sense and stretch your team without breaking them. Then evolve as you go. Use what you learn about yourself, your team, and your target to make the micro adjustments that improve execution and deliver results. Evaluate your own team and processes using The RACE Method. And don't forget to reach out if you need some help. (Chris@InfluenceLeadership.com)

CHAPTER 9

DEVELOPED

"Without continual growth and progress, such words as improvement, achievement, and success have no meaning."

—BENJAMIN FRANKLIN

I t's always interesting to try to imagine what the future will bring. *The Jetsons* cartoon show, based in the year 2062, envisioned a future where robots do all the housework, cars fold up to the size of a briefcase, and much of what we need is automated. We've got forty more years to see how that turns out. The movie *Bladerunner*, set in 2019, envisioned a future where rogue replicants were virtually indistinguishable from humans. *Back to the Future II,* set in 2015, predicted hover cars, self-lacing Nikes, and food rehydrators. The film *2001: A Space Odyssey* predicted a colonized moon by 2001.

While predictions of the future are often wrong, what we know is that the present will change dramatically in a short period of time. The more technology advances, the more the business environment must advance with it. If you aren't paying attention, you may just get left behind. Consider this list of things that didn't exist sixteen years ago:

- iPhone
- Facebook
- YouTube
- Twitter
- Instagram
- iPad
- Netflix streaming
- Google Maps
- Snapchat
- Spotify

- Android
- Uber
- Lyft
- Alexa
- Airbnb
- App Store
- Google Chrome
- WhatsApp
- Fitbit
- Waze

- Slack
- Square
- Dropbox
- Pinterest
- Venmo
- Bitcoin
- Hulu
- Kindle

Chances are you've used at least half of these in the last week. If we were to try to predict a list like this for the next fifteen years, there's no telling what it would look like. These market disruptors have changed the way we live, work, do business, and interact with people around the world.

> Change is inevitable and you can either get left behind or develop a plan for growth that puts you in the best place for success.

The lesson for an InSPIRED leader is this: change is inevitable and you can either get left behind or develop a plan for growth that puts you in the best place for success. If you stand still, you'll be outpaced rather quickly. But if you're nimble enough to move wisely with the changing times, you are in a position to grow with them.

You don't have to predict the future or recognize the next big thing. You simply have to be ready when your opportunity comes. You do that by developing a plan for growth. That's the D in the InSPIRED Pathway—commit to the process of being Developed.

DEVELOP OR DIE

There's a mistaken notion that being busy is the same thing as being productive. It's the tyranny of the urgent in action. By responding to the urgent, we tend to neglect the really important things in life—production capacity, personal growth, striving to make a difference, living a life of adventure, building a family, or crafting a leadership legacy.

In the movie *The Shawshank Redemption,* Red, "the guy who can get anything," says, "Get busy living, or get busy dying." In a counterintuitive way, busyness may seem productive, but it can actually be a distraction that slows you down. When you don't invest time to put first things first, you'll fall behind faster and struggle to catch up.

The truth is many people don't know how to adapt when things change, so they remain still, embracing the madness they know. However, nothing in life remains still. If you're not intentionally growing, developing, and moving, you're not standing still—you're getting left behind.

I've spent my fair share of time in airports around the world. Have you ever paid attention to what happens when you step on one of the "moving sidewalks" between concourses? These giant conveyor belts run silently in the floor, moving people along at about 1.4 miles per hour. The average person walking briskly (as you might expect in an airport) moves at about 3 miles per hour. So, if a person walks onto a moving sidewalk and continues a normal stride, he or she can go farther, faster.

When you stop, you stagnate.

But consider this. Suppose you and a friend are walking through the concourse together at a steady 3 miles an hour clip trying to make a connecting flight. Your friend jumps on the moving sidewalk and keeps walking at his normal pace. You stop to find something in your carry-on, figuring you'll just catch up in a minute. But when you look up, you can't even see your friend in the crowd ahead. He's gone, and you've been left behind.

Unfortunately, many people make this same mistake in leadership. They set aside intentional development and think they can just catch up later. But when you stop, you stagnate. Stagnate long enough and you'll die. There is no standing still in life. You're either moving forward or falling behind.

Now, to be clear, I'm not advocating hustle and grind 24/7 with no rest or relaxation. I'm advocating an intentional, holistic plan for developing every day in the midst of executing with excellence. We can't live in either ditch. We need results for today *and* results for tomorrow. Don't neglect it. Otherwise, the world will pass you by, and you'll wonder where everybody went.

CHOOSE TO DEVELOP

One of the unfortunate side effects of technology and our society is the inability to let things develop. We see something we want—and we want it now. But that's not the way growth works. In *First Things First,* Stephen R. Covey explains the principle of the farm. There is a time to plant, a time to fertilize and nurture, a time to grow, and a time to harvest. It's the way crops have grown for centuries. It's not negotiable. If a farmer fails to take the right action at the right time, the process doesn't work. If the ground isn't prepared, the seeds can't take root. If the seeds aren't planted, no plants can grow. If the plants don't grow, there is no harvest. The first step in the process is to decide that you will do what it takes and invest the time required to reap a harvest of growth so you and your team can continue to develop.

Develop is an interesting word. By definition, it means allowing something to happen over time. If you're old enough to remember a time before you carried a digital camera in your pocket, you may remember taking film to be developed. A hundred years ago, that process involved a darkroom, stinky chemicals, and a clothesline where prints could dry. That evolved to mini-canisters of 35-millimeter film to drop off for a machine to develop. You'd return a few hours later to pick up your prints (hoping that someone was smiling and no one blinked in at least one of the twenty-four pictures you shot). Now you can see those pictures instantly, delete, retake, and crop as needed. Nothing needs to develop. But people and processes are not photographs. Growth is not instant.

As a leader, you must invest time and make a conscious decision to develop. That means recognizing there's always room for growth. It means steadily looking for ways to improve. It means giving yourself permission to make mistakes with the understanding that every failure can push you forward if you are willing to learn. Choosing to develop means you embrace a growth mindset, where you continually strive to get better day by day.

The InSPIRED leader must make this choice every day: will I grow or drift? Will I choose excellence or mediocrity? Will I be a trendsetter or get left behind while digging through my luggage? It really does come down to a develop-or-die mentality. Leaders are learners, or else leaders aren't leaders for long. Organizations are doomed to mediocrity without a high-performing team. You can't have a high-performing team if you or your individual team members are unwilling to grow.

YOUR GROWTH MINDSET

To become an InSPIRED leader, you need a growth mindset. When you develop a growth mindset, you implement good habits that continually push you in the right direction. If you've ever tried to exercise to lose weight or gain muscle, you know it's easy to keep eating the way you've been eating or not to do the hard work of exercising. But that's not where growth happens. You start to lose weight when you put down the cookies and pick up the salad. You burn fat when you get off the couch and start jogging. You build muscle when you pick up the weights and lift until you're spent. Growth happens in uncomfortable places.

The same is true for growing as a leader. It doesn't matter if you're a ground-level employee just getting started or a C-Suite leader, there's always room to push forward, to choose *diligence in developing*. With a growth mindset, you're never fully developed. There is always uncharted ground to explore. Each time you hit a goal, you ask, "What's my new and higher goal?" You may reach the summit, but that doesn't mean your growth stops.

It's one thing to get to the top. It's another thing to stay on top. You must pay the price for excellence every day. For example, experts in the

> Continued growth is the price each of us must pay to achieve remarkable results on an ongoing basis.

industry have told me that most of what engineering students learn in year one of their studies is obsolete by the time they graduate. Does that mean students should give up and stop developing? Of course not. They are learning how to learn so they can stay up-to-date as technology and information changes. Even the act of learning forms new neural pathways in the brain. Continued growth is the price each of us must pay to achieve remarkable results on an ongoing basis.

But so few people are willing to do it. According to a 2018 Pew Research study, 24% of American adults haven't read a book in the last year.[16] Why? Many people operate under the belief that they've learned enough. Unfortunately, today's excellent will become tomorrow's average and the next day's failure. When you raise the bar on growth and development, you lift up your team and your organization. Then nobody gets left behind.

GROWTH BY DEGREES

How do you get better every single day? Individually, you need a personal growth plan. Organizationally, you need a developmental plan to grow your people every day.

When you make this investment in yourself and your people, you create champions. Champions are created through blood, sweat, and tears in the dark of night when nobody else is paying the price. Then the ring recognizes you as a champion. Champions pay the price, every single day. No one merely defaults to excellence. You elevate to excellence through diligent development and growth.

Growth happens by degrees. It can be tempting to want to grow too far, too fast, but that dangerous mindset leads to frustration and tragedy. It's similar to reaching the summit of Everest. Nobody goes from normal day-to-day life to base camp then to the summit in a few days. It's not possible. Everyone must acclimatize to prepare to meet the challenges ahead. At each stage of the journey, the climber must reach the limits, plateau and adjust, then push higher. Occasionally, he or she may need to fall back and regroup or even repeat the process until ready to make a run for the summit.

So, yes, growth happens by degrees, and you never know which degree will push you over the top. At 211 degrees, water is just really hot.

At 212 degrees it boils. That's when steam can power locomotives to pull heavy loads to new places, but not one degree before.

It doesn't matter where you are now; when you focus on getting one degree better each day, you grow—and growth compounds. Like an avalanche builds momentum as it slides down the mountainside, your good growth habits compound as you build momentum.

I often do an exercise in my training sessions where I ask participants to list their knowns and the unknowns. They take a piece of paper and draw a line right down the middle. On the left side, they list all their knowns. On the right side, they list all their unknowns. The knowns are all the things they know about or know how to do. The unknowns are all the things they are uncertain about or would like to know how to do. It's the space between those two where they can plan their growth.

Growth moves an unknown to a known. If you're content to live on the left side of the page—with what you already know—you're stagnating. It's only when you find and pursue the next best iteration of you that you can take the right steps to elevate your leadership.

You have to examine where you want to go and visualize your summit. Then you can get real about where you are now and begin to plan the moves to close the gap. That's your growth plan. That's what you need to do daily.

Don't worry about the size of the gap for now. Remember, growth happens by degrees, not in giant leaps and bounds. In fact, the more you grow, the smaller each growth increment might feel. That's okay. Start to focus on the space between the knowns and the unknowns and develop goals to move you to take the next best step.

RACE-READY GOALS

My wife and I decided we wanted to hike a 10K. But not just any hike. This hike was in China. And it wasn't just any place in China, it was at the Great Wall of China. Being the adventure seeker I am, I didn't want to see the Great Wall from the same perspective as everyone else. So, I arranged to start the hike in a village north of the typical tourist area of the wall.

We started way back in the rural areas, then hiked up to the wall before starting. In the broken, crumbly parts of the wall, we had to navigate some tricky footing. My legs were screaming as I used my going-down-the-Great-Wall-muscles to maintain my footing. I hadn't built up those particular muscles well prior to the adventure because I didn't realize I would need them. I wasn't race-ready.

One of the most important things to remember about the Developed piece of the InSPIRED Pathway is you have to get *race-ready* to grow. But you can't get race-ready if you don't plan for the race. That's why so many people struggle when they get a promotion. It's not that they don't want to be promoted, they just aren't ready for what they find when they get there. Then they don't make a plan with race-ready goals to close the gap.

One of the best ways to do this is to develop goals using the proven SMART (Specific, Measurable, Attainable, Realistic, and Time-bound) acrostic. To begin, you've got to make your goals **Specific.** If you aim at nothing in particular, you'll hit it every time. Many people have a general idea to grow and develop, but no specific idea of what that development should look like. That's a surefire way to wander in the wilderness of mediocrity. The difference between a lamp and a laser is focus. A laser can do incredible things with concentrated power. If you want to develop, you've got to be laser-focused.

Once you have a specific goal in mind, you need to make it **Measurable.** Suppose you wanted to become a million-dollar salesperson. That's specific, but is it measurable? It can be if you break that larger goal down into smaller pieces. You could divide a million dollars by the number of days you work in the year, then figure out how many dollars per day it will take to get there. You could break it down into the number of sales leads and track your progress in that way. When you break things down into measurable increments, you get smaller, measurable checkpoints so the journey feels less overwhelming.

Goals also need to be **Attainable.** It's great to want to be the CEO, but if you are the front line worker at General Motors, you're not going to become the CEO next year. If you haven't exercised since high school, you aren't going to run a marathon next weekend. If you are that frontline worker, your attainable goal may be to take some leadership classes and put yourself on the radar of your supervisors for a leadership position. If you've been sitting on the couch, your attainable goal may be to sign up for a 5K and train for the next six weeks.

You also have to make your goals **Realistic**. If you're just starting out in sales with no connections, and the current best salesperson is doing half a million in sales each year, your million dollar sales goal may not be realistic—for this year. It's great to have huge goals. But if they are unrealistic, you'll get frustrated and quit. Make your goals a stretch but keep them realistic to achieve sustainable success.

Finally, you've got to make your goals **Time-bound.** If you leave the time component open-ended, it's like running a race with a moving finish line. You'll just keep kicking the goal further down the line without ever making progress. Most people need a deadline to get things done; that's why eBay auctions have timers! Tying your goals to a specific time lets you envision the end and take the necessary steps to get there.

INVEST IN YOURSELF.
INVEST IN YOUR TEAM.

If you want to go from where you are—as an individual or an organization—to where you want to be, you must pay the price and delineate the steps. Growth doesn't come for free. Begin by answering these questions:

- Are you passionate about growth?

- Are you worth the investment?

- Is your organization worth investing in?

I'm continually amazed at how many people think they can get a return on something in which they've never invested. The best companies invest around 3% of their revenue into growing people. If you want to elevate, you must take the initiative and invest in growth. If you don't value growth (or you don't value yourself), then you won't be keen on investing in it.

Back in the early 1990s, I made the decision to work with a leadership group out of Tulsa, Oklahoma. I actually moved our family from Dallas/ Fort Worth to Tulsa and interned for a leader named Jim for about eight or nine months. Jim was the first person to put a John Maxwell book in my hand and helped initiate my growth track. He was running a nonprofit touching about 5,000 people on a weekly basis.

It was a sacrifice for me to move my family and be mentored by him. But it was a sacrifice I was willing to make to reach my long-term growth goals. The leader I am today is based on the sacrifices I made then. I learned lessons that helped me become a mentor to other leaders and that paid dividends for the rest of my life.

> The fruit in your life today comes from the price you paid yesterday.

The fruit in your life today comes from the price you paid yesterday. The leader you're going to be a year from now is based on what you do over the next twelve months. I want to give you permission right now to invest in yourself. What about you? Do you have an investment budget for your growth? Do you have an investment budget for your team? If not, you should. You will become what you are investing in for the next twelve to thirty-six months.

LEADERS: MODEL GROWTH

As a leader, are you modeling a growth state or maintaining the status quo? Are you modeling an investment state of paying the price for future success or are you letting the tyranny of the urgent rule the day? Only six percent of leaders rated themselves as "very ready" for the next five years.[17] Are you very ready? Do you even know what's coming? Are you investing now to prepare for what will happen then?

> You'll never develop into the leader you can be, the leader you were meant to be, unless you are willing to pay the price for growth.

Leaders, you're responsible for the culture of your organization. You have to put into the organization what it's going to need for the future. You have to guide them from the current state to the future state. As a leader, you grow to bridge that chasm with growth, learning, culture, experience, mentorship, and coaching.

When you invest in your team, you equip, empower, delineate, delegate, elevate, and inspire them to be better. Three to five years from now, when you're dominating the market, your team's amazing impact will be your ROI. You deserve *that* team. But if you fail to invest in yourself and your team, you'll also deserve what comes your way in three to five years. Your good players will leave, your bad players will stay, and your results will be anything but inspiring.

Your people are worth the price. You are worth the price. Your future state is worth the investment. You'll never develop into the leader you can be, the leader you were meant to be, unless you are willing to pay the price for growth.

Development takes time, but time passes no matter what you do. Use it well. Make being Developed a high, ongoing priority and you'll be ready to enjoy InSPIRED success and with remarkable results.

TOOL KIT

Summary

- While the predictions of the future are often wrong, what is right is that things in the present can and will change *dramatically* in a short period of time.

- The lesson for an InSPIRED leader is this: you can either get left behind when things change or develop a plan for growth that puts you in the best place for success.

- The point is not where you are in relation to everyone else. The point is that when you stop, you stagnate, and when you stagnate you ultimately die.

- When you develop a growth mindset you implement good habits that continually push you and your team in the right direction.

- Without growth and development, you'll soon realize that today's excellence becomes tomorrow's standard. And tomorrow's standard will be the next day's mediocrity.

- Growth happens by degrees, and you never know which degree will push you over the success edge.

- The fruit of your life today is built on the price that you paid yesterday.

Startling Statistics

- 24% of American adults haven't read a book in the last year.

Action Steps

- **Decide to develop.** InSPIRED leaders aren't content to stay where they are, because they know they have room to improve. But without a conscious decision to develop, they will actually regress. Make a commitment now that you will develop. You won't stay still. You will strive to be the best version of you that you can possibly be.

- **Plan for growth.** Growth doesn't just happen. It requires planning. But first, it requires an awareness of who you are, who you aren't, and who you could become. List your strengths and weaknesses, areas in which you should improve, areas you should avoid, your personal finish line, and some checkpoints along the way. Your plan will need to be continually refined, but having a plan is the first step to growth.

- **Budget for investment.** Personal development comes with a cost, including time and money. Decide what percentage of your income or budget you'll allocate to growth and set it aside. Do the same for your time. Put growth on your calendar so it will stay a priority.

CHAPTER 10

InSPIRED CULTURE

"The first step in changing a culture, I believe, starts with the senior leadership team—and with the CEO."

—DENISE MORRISON

When you think about companies with notable cultures, which ones come to mind? Is it Southwest Airlines with the late maverick Herb Kelleher at the helm, boldly forging his own path against a sea of uniformity? Or is it Zappos, the online shoe retailer who takes culture so seriously that employees literally write the book on culture each year. Zappos even has a "cultural fit" interview as part of the hiring process.

Maybe you think of Pixar where team members are encouraged to engage in creativity and whimsy. Or perhaps Google, where employees are encouraged to work 20% of their time on personal projects, projects which often become a valuable part of the Google business model. Maybe you think of Patagonia where employees are encouraged to invest in causes they care about. Or Chick-fil-A, where many of the high school kids who work their first jobs end up earning scholarships and returning to manage or run their own restaurants.

The organizations all have unique cultures that dictate how they function and how effective they can be. And so it is with you and your team or organization. Culture is the collective processes you use to get work done, and includes the reality of the integrated relationships governing those processes. The hard part is that culture often seems intangible until it goes awry and manifests itself in a concrete way.

As much as the word is referred to in a corporate mission statement, companies intentional about culture are exceedingly rare. That rarity is ironic when you consider the Latin origins of the word, which means "to tend, cultivate, or grow." If you've ever maintained a garden, or even a decent lawn, you know things tend toward disorder and chaos when left alone. In organizations, culture is made up of hundreds of big and little things that blend together to create the essence of who and what a company is. If left alone, culture defaults to the whim or personality of the strongest or most intense people—not by design, but by default.

> Culture is the culmination of your past, the reality of your present, and the prediction of your future.

Culture establishes the company's collective beliefs, language, and behaviors. In turn, these internal elements affect every aspect of The InSPIRED Pathway. The culture permeates the environment with an underlying set of ground rules and overarching set of expectations that frame the mindset of each employee. In short, culture is the culmination of your past, the reality of your present, and the prediction of your future.

ENTER, LEADERSHIP

Great cultures don't just happen. They are a natural outflow of leadership—from those who founded the company to the current leaders. It is a direct reflection of the leadership style that is promoted and fostered. How those leaders operate or have operated became the expected norms. Those norms created the collective culture. As a leader, it is your responsibility to lead where the organization needs to go. How do you do that? By intentionally *building* your culture.

Culture starts transferring within the first fifteen minutes of a new hire experiencing your organization. The first interactions they see or experience start shaping their beliefs about what *normal* behavior looks like, what is accepted and what gets critiqued. Every person brings his or her hopes, dreams, and expectations on that first day. Then reality and expectations collide, leading either to fulfillment or frustration.

> Great cultures are a natural outflow of leadership—from those who founded the company to the current leaders.

You might think about it like a major interstate with all the traffic flowing together. When a newbie is dumped into that mix and sees how everybody else is driving, he or she starts driving in similar ways. The onboarding process is where it's critical to teach the collective behaviors of the organization. The scary thing is how often people jump into ineffective cultures and simply copy the behavior modeled for them.

For example, in some dysfunctional cultures, employees learn right away to copy everybody on email so they don't get hung out to dry. It's the "cover your backside at all times" mentality. Or when the leader says he wants collaboration and opinion, but what he really wants you to do is be quiet and take orders. People learn quickly. All of these things contribute to how your organization operates and collectively become the culture.

Every interaction—and I do mean every interaction—adds to what it means to be a part of the organizational *family.* Culture is not defined by the posters on your walls, but by the chatter in your halls.

THE POWER OF INSPIRED CULTURES

If you've had the privilege of working in an InSPIRED culture, you've already experienced some of its benefits. But you may not have realized how deeply this kind of culture can impact the entire organization.

In my years of working with companies and helping them build InSPIRED cultures, here are some of the benefits I've discovered. InSPIRED culture...

- **Attracts the best talent.** Talent always has a choice. Especially in today's highly mobile work environment, the best people can go anywhere to work for anyone. So why would they choose you? A healthy culture produces all the intangible quality-of-life benefits that top talent demands. Even if they may be able to make more money elsewhere, they're more likely to join a team where they like the leader, are treated fairly, and feel connected to a sense of purpose.

- **Maximizes the best talent.** A healthy culture is a pro-growth culture that seeks to empower everyone on the team to deliver his or her best in the areas of their greatest strengths. If you think it's too much trouble to maximize your current talent, try not doing it. You'll soon be left with only the employees who lack both the skills needed at present and the ambition to grow in the future. Not good.

- **Retains the best talent.** According to the Qualtrics Global Employee Pulse 2017 study, "employees with a high confidence level in their company's senior leadership are five times as likely to remain with their employer more than 2 years compared to employees with no confidence." It's that simple. If your people believe in you as a leader, they'll stay. If not, they're five times as likely to leave.

- **Increases productivity.** When your employees are engaged, you'll get more done with fewer people because you won't be carrying the weight of disengaged employees. At the end of the day, a healthy culture grows the bottom line (and possibly, your own performance bonus).

- **Frees you to focus on the future.** It's amazing how proactive you can be about tomorrow when you're not having to put out fires today.

Imagine for a moment that in your particular sphere of influence you create a thriving culture where people are happy to come to work. They love their jobs and are proud of the work they do. They push each other to greatness and, as a result, they execute with excellence. People are real with each other, because they are living with authenticity. They follow their passions, because you've put them in the right seat on the bus. They serve one another, because they know a rising tide lifts all boats. And they aren't stagnant, because you've created a plan to help them develop and grow.

Do you think a team like that would get noticed in your organization? You bet.

INTENTIONAL CULTURE

An InSPIRED culture takes work to make it a reality. It should come as no surprise that the first step to an InSPIRED culture is the same as the first step to becoming an InSPIRED leader, and that means getting *intentional.*

Right now, you have a culture, but it may be by default, not by design. With a designed culture, you *determine* what your reputation will be. You create key descriptors that describe who you are. You develop a code of conduct. You control the internal and external chatter. You determine that your brand will be good as gold and able to be counted on to deliver superior service and remarkable results.

You get intentional by engaging the three pieces of the process: Discover, Design, and Build. Intentionality starts with getting clear about the culture you have (Discover), then choosing the culture you want (Design), *before* working to create that culture going forward (Build).

To build an InSPIRED culture you have to be intentional about two things: what you're moving away from and what you're running towards—the push *and* the pull. The Discover phase is all about figuring out where you are now so you know what the push factors are. The Design phase is where you get clarity about the cultural summit you're aspiring to reach. Only then can you fully engage the adventure to build your culture.

DISCOVER: WHAT CULTURE DO YOU HAVE NOW?

The first step is to discover exactly where your culture is now so you can diagnose a solution. Your present culture is getting you the results you're experiencing right now. That's the reality of your current state. So, if you had to describe your culture in ten words or phrases, what would those descriptors be?

You may start by identifying which areas in your team are causing pain—*the push factors.* These friction points keep you from operating at your best. It may be a faulty system that slows down productivity. It may be a poor relationship that adds toxicity to the group. It may be you've reached capacity and can't increase output without adding more resources. Whatever these pain points are, you've got to identify them before you can fix them.

This Discover phase requires asking hard questions about what the company leadership values, the marketplace, and your unique approach to—well, everything. Here are three high-level questions to get you started:

1. What does it look and feel like to be our employee? (Engaged Operational Excellence)

2. How does our internal culture ripple out to our external customers? And is that a good or bad thing? (Inspired Customer Service)

3. Is our integrated culture delivering results that return appropriate value to our investors? (ROI)

Then you can dig deeper into the DITLO. Culture quickly trains each person as to what's acceptable on a daily basis. So, as a leader you've got to be intentional and think about how *we* function in your organization. What leaders expect and inspect, how leaders lead, how they are experienced in every interaction, outflows into their direct reports—all of this establishes a series of expectations and behaviors which become the operational norm known as *culture.*

- Start digging deeper with these questions:

- Are we inspirational or exasperational?

- Are you a culture of *owners* or *victims?*

- Are we intentional or accidental, "on point" or "on fire"?

- What does our service look like—both internal and external?

- Are we passion-fueled contributors or check-cashing zombies?

- How do we integrate or deeply interact with others?

- Are we real and authentic in our relationships with empathy, care, and EQ?

- Are you *functional* or *dysfunctional?*

- Are we equipped and empowered to execute with excellence or dumbed down and micromanaged where most underperform and excuse with complacency?

- Are you a culture of *excellence* or *excuses?*

- Are we *do what I say* leaders? Or... *I believe you are an amazing contributor. Use your best judgment leaders?*

- Are we diligently developing daily or are our glory days behind us?

- Are we satisfied with yesterday's leftovers slathered with a healthy layer of malaise?

Once you've discovered the state of your culture now, you can begin intentionally designing a new, inspired culture based on your shared passion and purpose.

For more help assessing your organizational culture and special offers. visit:

InspiredLeadership.com/Assessments

DECIDE: WHAT CULTURE DO YOU WANT?

If you were scaling Everest, your destination would be obvious—the summit. In the Iditarod dog race in Alaska, the finish line is clear. In the America's Cup competition, the objective is pretty straightforward. Not so much with culture. You have to decide what kind of culture you want before you can build it. That means you have to resist the tyranny of the urgent long enough to create and cast a vision for an inspired culture that works for your organization.

So what kind of culture do you want? This vision for who you want to become is what can move you to a better place—the *pull* factor. This dual focus is critical for growth. It requires you to look at how things *could be* if you made adjustments. All great leaders keep one eye on where they are now and one eye on where they are going in the future.

If you inherited a team and were asked to change how they operated, you were, in essence, asked to change the culture. To do so, you need to establish a cultural standard that inspires the team to behave and produce in a new way. A cultural standard is a picture of the future state. It's the *best-in-class* vision of how you want life within your team or organization to look and feel. If you hope to get maximum engagement and effectiveness from your team, you have to have a defined, articulated, communicated standard to which you can hold people accountable.

In my keynotes and seminars, I tell the tongue-in-cheek story of setting a cultural standard for my teenage boys. If you're a parent, you likely have experience with this. Teenage boys can be a handful at times, and mine have become great men. But when they were finding their way during their teen years, I was determined to set a standard. After some poor choices on one particularly trying day, I sat them down and said:

I'm not sure if you are aware of this, but you are wearing my last name. I don't want that behavior attached to the Fuller name. Reputations can take hold fast and linger long. So, you have two options: change your behavior or change your last name. I'll still love you just as much—but I don't want that behavior attached to my last name.

Just imagine if you held yourself to such high standards within your organization that no one wanted to do anything to damage the brand's name! Perhaps it might help to think of it this way: what if your culture was truly represented by the reviews and comments on Glassdoor?

In the Decide phase, you'll want to revisit all of the diagnostic questions you asked in the Discover phase, but with a positive spin. Instead of asking how things are, imagine how things could be. What might be possible? What would *best case* look and feel like?

Start by re-engaging your purpose and getting clear on what you value. A tech startup may value innovation, moving quickly to market, trying and failing fast, and learning from the process. Other companies may move more methodically, with leadership valuing steady growth and a proven process. Neither culture is right or wrong, and both can work—if the right people buy in.

Once you decide what you want your culture to be, you're ready to get intentional about building that culture in an InSPIRED fashion.

BUILD: HOW WILL YOU CREATE AN INSPIRED CULTURE?

It all starts with being intentional. You cannot complain about what you permit. You endorse what you allow. Therefore, culture begins with you as a leader. You have to start by creating a localized culture first. Then, like ripples in a pond, the small changes start to build momentum and move out from there. When you make your department shine, you become a case study. Instead of pushing your culture on others, they pull from what they see in you. Small steps— done the right way—can lead to big changes.

Once you've got a vision for how things could be, you can create a model for repeatable, sustainable, and scalable growth, including operations and relationships. Remember, a leader's job is to deliver results.

After sketching out what you want your Intentional culture to be, the next phase is to assemble a plan for cultural transformation. You'll need to establish new norms via practical daily habits and clear expectations, breaking everything into easily actionable behaviors that can be reinforced through positive accountability.

The good news is that the same path you follow to become an InSPIRED leader can also be applied to building an InSPIRED culture. And wherever you find yourself in your organization, you have the power to influence others above or below you on the org chart.

There's no need to reinvent the wheel here. If you can find awesome and copy it, do it. Is someone already championing the kind of culture you want? Maybe you can "borrow" from another leader inside your organization or from another organization that has a great culture. It's not difficult to find information on great cultures and how they work. Research your competitors, other industries that are nothing like yours, and delve into your own experience to assemble a clear picture of your ideal culture.

Most importantly, you must give people a new language to use to talk about the new culture. Culture is driven by the language we speak. Those words generate beliefs that produce actionable outputs.

The new nomenclature must become embedded within the day-to-day communication of the team. A new day in your culture requires new, inspired words.

For example, if you employ the InSPIRED Pathway with your team, you'll start saying things like:

- "The only way we can begin telling a new, inspired story is if we have inspired relationships with our clients."

- "To have inspired relationships, we need to get intentional about providing inspired service."

- "Is our inspired story driven by passion and purpose? If not, how can we reconnect with it and get energized about it?"

- "Does this client align with our ideal client avatar so that we know we can engage in an inspired relationship or should we pass on the opportunity?"

- "Is there a clear deliverable on which we can execute with excellence for that client? If not, are we setting ourselves up for delivering less than inspired service?"

- "How well integrated is a potential client when it comes to getting things done? How well will we integrate with them?"

All of the components in the InSPIRED Pathway factor into this new language you and your team will begin to speak. As that language gets embedded deeper and deeper into your organizational psyche, it naturally shapes beliefs and flows out in actions.

After determining the language you need to embed into conversations, the next step is to empower your people to give their best efforts by giving them permission to act on their best judgment. Building an inspired culture means you empower people to work in and through their areas of passion. You put them in the right place to succeed and equip them with everything they need to do their jobs well.

That sounds a lot simpler than it is. Once again, it requires intentional focus and action. And if I can be of any help to you in rolling out an InSPIRED culture in your organization, just let me know.

UNDERSTAND THE RESISTANCE

Change doesn't come easily. Implementing a new culture can feel a bit like turning the Titanic. That's why you shouldn't be surprised when you meet resistance. There will be laggards who don't like the changes and can't see past the *here* and *now.* Early adopters will jump on board immediately and embrace the change. For those who do, celebrate their behaviors as the new normal. What gets rewarded gets repeated. Keep in mind that not everyone will be the right fit for the new culture—and that's okay.

Change offers you a prime opportunity to lead and coach the people who struggle with it. If you know your people well, it won't be difficult to see who will struggle to adapt to the culture you want. Create a plan for them to become their best and fit the new mindset. Demonstrate how serving others on the team helps them do their jobs better. Show how breaking down silos and miscommunication leads to seamless integration and increased productivity. Inspired service means inspired customer relationships that make their days brighter and jobs easier. It also means building real, authentic relationships, because authenticity builds trust—and trust is the currency you need to lead the change to an InSPIRED culture.

When rolling out a new culture, you need to make sure every member of your team is fully Integrated. The best way to integrate is to work from both the top-down and the bottom-up. Organizational buy-in begins at the top. Make sure the leaders on your team understand the fullness of the culture changes, so they don't unintentionally counteract its adoption. When they are clear on the new culture, they can begin to let its effects trickle down through the team. Cascading implementation ensures buy-in at every level. And when each level begins to implement these culture changes, it allows critical conversations to take place on that specific level. Then the people at that level can be empowered to deal with level-specific issues as they adopt the culture in that department.

As you prepare to execute, ask these questions:

- Who are the key stakeholders?

- Which ones will be impacted the most?

- Who are the "swing dogs" you must convert first?

- Who will struggle the most? The least?

- Who will need coaching?

- Which channel or department will struggle the most? The least?

- Is there a channel we should implement changes in first?

The answers to these questions can help guide the rollout process and identify potential pain points in each channel. Then you can discuss solutions for these pinch points on the front end. Anticipating problems and having solutions ready demonstrates good leadership and awareness of your team. Then schedule implementation debriefs at regular intervals or checkpoints to keep small concerns from becoming big issues. Dealing with problems as they arise keeps everyone up to speed and on board.

It will take time to change the culture, so you'll need to be patient with the process. Build in time to create conversation around the desired vision and let your people talk it through. They need to internalize the vision before they can manifest the results.

It's also critical to include as many people as possible on the front end. If you come out of your office like an oracle with a vision and start turning everyone's world upside down, people are probably going to react poorly. (Wouldn't you?) But if you get feedback and buy-in on the front end, people will feel like they're a part of positive change.

In the Iditarod race I mentioned earlier, the swing dogs are the influencers that impact the entire team. In implementing an InSPIRED culture you've got to include the swing dogs on your cultural change efforts. These influential team members aren't always in a position of leadership, but they are major influencers. They have the power to turn resistors to the cause into champions for the cause. See what they like about the plan. See where they push back. Ask them to point out implementation issues. Then heed their advice. They are often the ones who can make or break the culture change.

By including your team, you leverage their strengths to bring about cultural change. The new inspired culture will feel natural to them, because it was done with them in mind.

WHAT'S YOUR ESPRIT DE CORPS?

As we began our InSPIRED leadership journey together, you met Matt who was on his way to becoming a zombie in the workplace. He was overwhelmed, overworked, and underprepared. He was reacting to a company culture that was draining him and damaging his family. But it doesn't have to be that way—for him or you.

Imagine what your organization could look like if your culture were rich, vibrant, and inspired! What if you were surrounded by fully engaged and passionate people who loved their work and workplace? What if they went home each day better people than when they arrived? What if their families noticed a difference and started living better lives, too? What if they bought into the InSPIRED adventure and were excited to do work that mattered—all the way from the front line to the C-Suite?

This vision isn't fantasy. I've helped countless organizations achieve it as leaders have decided to embrace the adventure and change the status quo. They get Intentional about where they are and where they want to go. They reacquire a heart to Serve, embrace their Passions, and help their teams do the same. They create processes that lead to Integration, both internally and externally. They are Real in their relationships; they want results but not at the expense of their employees' souls. So, they Execute with excellence and watch their employees thrive. Then they build a plan for growth and Development that ensures people not only work and earn a living, but also thrive and feel rewarded. They grow, and as they grow, the organization grows with them.

It's not a dream, it's a reality for many organizations. Follow The InSPIRED Leadership Pathway and soon you too will transform ordinary into extraordinary and achieve remarkable results. If I can be of any help to you, your team, or organization, I invite you to reach out and start the conversation at InfluenceLeadership.com, explore our RightPath assessments at InspiredLeadership.com/Assessements, or shoot me a personal note at Chris@InfluenceLeadership.com.

TOOL KIT

Summary

- Culture is a critical part of any organization, and one that often seems intangible until it goes awry.

- Culture must be cultivated if it is to bring out the best in your organization.

- A healthy culture is a pro-growth culture that seeks to empower everyone on the team to deliver his or her best in the areas of greatest strengths.

- Intentionality starts when you are clear about the culture you have and you get clear about the kind of culture you want.

- All great leaders keep one eye on where they are now and one eye on where they are going in the future. This dual focus is critical for growth.

- Authenticity builds trust and trust is the currency of an InSPIRED culture.

- Without strong relationships and clear communication, your team will never give you their best. Good culture builds strong relationships.

- Good cultures don't just extract from their team members, they add to their team members.

Action Steps

- **Evaluate your culture.** Culture runs quietly in the background, but influences every facet of your organization. Take some time to grade your culture. Start with the culture inside your immediate team and move outward to the organization. Use The InSPIRED Pathway as a guide to evaluate where your culture is working for you and where it's working *against* you. Visit InspiredLeadership.com/Assessments and take the Inspired Culture assessment.

- **Anticipate the problems.** To be clear, people aren't problems, but some will embrace culture change more readily than others. Identify who will embrace the change and who will need some encouragement. Then develop a plan to get both types of people involved in the culture change. Decide who needs coaching and then determine how to do it.

- **Enlist the swing dogs.** Culture changes fastest when everyone is on board. Think about your team and determine who will be the biggest influencers. Then think about the order in which you should unveil the cultural changes. Get as many people involved as possible, but do it in a methodical way for the greatest success and least resistance.

ACKNOWLEDGEMENTS

Some of the people who have InSPIRED me along the way:

Robin: My amazing wife—thank you for doing doing all that you do! It has made it easier to pursue my passion of making a difference in this world!

Bill: More than a brother, you are a mentor and a benchmark. I am where I am, in large part, because of you.

Bill, Jesse, and the StoryBuilders team: You have helped shape my thoughts and fought through the struggles of this birthing process in the midst of tectonic business shifts while acquiring RightPath. You are resilient!

John Maxwell: Your imprint and mentorship started twenty-seven years ago. Partnering with you and everyone in the Corporate Learning divisions for the last fifteen years, we've won, we've learned, and we've made a lot of impact in leaders and organizations.

To my clients: There are too many of you to list. We have learned so much from each other. You have shaped me. As I have shared what I know, you have taught me. Together we have made a difference!

ABOUT THE AUTHOR

Chris Fuller is an International Leadership Speaker, Author, and Consultant with over 25 years of experience in many aspects of business and organizational effectiveness including Leadership Development, Culture, Strategy, Sales, Emotional Intelligence, and Team Effectiveness. Chris is Principal and Owner of RightPath Resources and Influence Leadership, Inc.

A born adventurer, Chris pulls leadership insights from his own adventures and weaves them into his teaching. He has delivered keynotes and facilitated strategic sessions for an impressive list of companies including Microsoft, Coca-Cola, Alvarez & Marsal, Dell Computers, Pfizer, State Farm Insurance, GAP, PricewaterhouseCoopers, Ascend Performance Materials, DOW Agrosciences, McDonald's, Lyondell-Basell, PC Connection, Compuware, Gulfstream, and Varde Partners. His experience in business and in working with such clients yields valuable, best-practice insights.

Chris has written two books. His breakout book Iditarod Leadership: Unleashing the Power of the Team, has been recognized by the Washington Post on Leadership with impact reaching people and companies in over 75 countries. A highly-sought-after speaker, consultant, and facilitator, Chris has traveled the world equipping leaders and organizations to execute with excellence and reach their summits.

Chris received his Bachelor's Degree in Accounting from The University of Texas at Arlington. For leisure, Chris enjoys SCUBA, sailing, fishing, music, motorsports, and has participated in skydiving, Alaskan dog mushing, and even made time to travel to Mt. Everest Base Camp to see the top of the world.

To learn more about Chris, visit InfluenceLeadership.com. To explore more about putting RightPath assessments to work for you and your organization, visit RightPath.com. To take advantage of the special offers found in this book, visit InspiredLeadership.com/Assessments.

Exclusive Offer to Readers

Take the next step to achieve remarkable results by taking advantage of the best personal and team assessments—at a substantial discount! Visit **InspiredLeadership.com/assessments** to claim your savings on these cutting edge diagnostic tools from RightPath:

THE RP 4/6 ASSESSMENT

The RightPath Path4 and Path6 behavioral assessments assist in identifying your personal hard-wiring and offer an in-depth display of your predictable natural behaviors.

THE 360° LEADERSHIP ASSESSMENT

The RightPath 360° assessment measures 64 key leadership traits, providing the unique, real-time, and personal feedback leaders need to maximize growth.

THE InSPIRED CULTURE ASSESSMENT

The InSPIRED OES Quick Assessment can help you formulate a base-line of your culture by intentionally capturing a clear picture and understanding of your present culture.

Visit InspiredLeadership.com/assessments
to claim your discounts now!

ENDNOTES

[1] Danielle Fritze, et al., *"Mind the Workplace"*, Mental Health America, 2017, http://www.mentalhealthamerica.net/sites/default/files/Mind%20the%20 Workplace%20-%20MHA%20Workplace%20Health%20Survey%202017%20 FINAL.pdf

[2] Broughton Coburn. *Everest: Mountain without Mercy.* (National Geographic Society, 1997), p 189.

[3] Graham Hays. "Central Washington offers the ultimate act of sportsmanship," College Sports, ESPN, April 28, 2008, http://www.espn.com/college-sports/ columns/story?columnist=hays_graham&id=3372631

[4] Carolyn Cutrone, "How To Get Customers To Become Advocates For Your Product," *Business Insider,* October 25, 2012, https://www.businessinsider. com/how-to-create-an-inspiring-brand-2012-10

[5] "destiny (n.)," *online etymology dictionary,* February 14, 2019, https://www. etymonline.com/word/destiny.

[6] "destiny (n.)," *online etymology dictionary,* February 14, 2019, https://www. etymonline.com/word/destination?ref=etymonline_crossreference

[7] Service Quality Institute, "Companies Don't See Reality In Their Service Reflection," March 21, 2013, https://www.customer-service.com/companies- dont-see-reality-in-their-service-reflection/

[8] Colleen DeBaise, "Stop Losing Money and Focus on Customer Service," Marketing, *Entrepreneur,* September 3, 2013, https://www.entrepreneur.com/ article/228129#ixzz2dtg5wBrf

[9] Marc Beaujean, Jonathan Davidson, and Stacey Madge, "The 'moment of truth' in customer service," McKinsey Quarterly, *McKinsey & Company,* February 2006, https://www.mckinsey.com/business-functions/organization/our-insights/the- moment-of-truth-in-customer-service

[10] Marcel Schwantes, "Research: Why 70 Percent of Employees Aren't Working to Their Full Potential Comes Down to 1 Simple Reason", *Lead,* Inc., November 22, 2017, https://www.inc.com/marcel-schwantes/research-why-70-percent- of-employees-arent-working-to-their-full-potential-comes-down-to-1-simple- reason.html

[11] Editors of Encyclopaedia Britannica, America's Cup: Yacht Race and Trophy," *Encyclopaedia Britannica*, Accessed on March 5, 2019, https://www.britannica.com/sports/Americas-Cup

[12] Pierre-Yves Hittelet, 12 Leadership Lessons to Learn from Navy SEALS, *Inc.* May 25, 2017, "https://www.inc.com/pierre-yves-hittelet/navy-seal-leadership-lessons.html

[13] Kendry Cherry, "What Is Gestalt Psychology?," Basics, *Very Well Mind,* October 5, 2018, https://www.verywellmind.com/what-is-gestalt-psychology-2795808

[14] Christine Porath and Christine Pearson, "The Price of Incivility," Motivating People, Harvard Business Review, January 2013, https://hbr.org/2013/01/the-price-of-incivility.

[15] PMI, "$1 Million Wasted Every 20 Seconds By Organizations Around The World", *PM Times,* Accessed March 5, 2019, https://www.projecttimes.com/articles/1-million-wasted-every-20-seconds-by-organizations-around-the-world.html

[16] Andrew Perrin, "Who doesn't read books in America?," FactTank, *Pew Research Center,* March 23, 2018, http://www.pewresearch.org/fact-tank/2018/03/23/who-doesnt-read-books-in-america/

[17] Michelle Riklan, "What Employers Look For in Future Leaders," CommunityVoice, *Forbes,* July 28, 2016, https://www.forbes.com/sites/forbescoachescouncil/2016/07/28/what-employers-look-for-in-future-leaders/#46008e464c5c

[18] Susan M. Heathfield, "Find Out How Zappos Reinforces Its Company Culture," Human Resources: Culture, *The Balance Careers,* September 21, 2008, https://www.thebalancecareers.com/zappos-company-culture-1918813

CPSIA information can be obtained
at www.ICGtesting.com
Printed in the USA
LVHW082010101220
673848LV00029B/749